# A COMPREHENSIVE GUIDE FOR PARENTING THE ADHD CHILD

*Paul Lavin, Ph.D.*

*Kathryn Lavin, M.A.*

PublishAmerica

Baltimore

First printing

ISBN: 1-4137-7578-0
PUBLISHED BY PUBLISHAMERICA, LLLP
www.publishamerica.com
Baltimore

Printed in the United States of America

# TABLE OF CONTENTS

# FOREWORD

This book focuses on attention deficit hyperactivity disorder (ADHD) and the importance of providing appropriate educational and mental health services in order to treat it. The efficacious treatment of ADHD children requires a team effort involving parents, teachers, physicians, and mental health professionals. Ongoing communication, close monitoring, and a consistent application and thorough assessment of those services which are provided are necessary ingredients for helping this oftentimes underserved population. No particular treatment modality has a monopoly on the successful treatment of ADHD. Rather, it is a combination of approaches which are carefully and skillfully designed and implemented that usually works best.

Many of the approaches presented and discussed in this book have been developed and put into practice at Norbel School, an educational facility specializing in working with ADHD and learning disabled children. The Norbel School staff utilizes a highly structured behavior modification system in which our children receive poker chips or points for engaging in appropriate "on-task" behavior. These, in turn, can be used by the students to purchase tangible rewards and privileges.

While applying behavior modification can work effectively in the classroom, we clearly recognize that the assistance of our parents is of the utmost importance in helping to make our program a successful one. After all, parents have the most influence on their child's development. As we all know, what happens at home can and often does have a marked impact on how the child behaves in the classroom.

With the preceding in mind, we have devised a number of behaviorally, cognitively, and affectively based programs that parents can put into practice with their ADHD child at home. These programs can easily be coordinated with the school, thereby making it even more likely that the youngster will profit from his or her educational experiences. It should be noted that school counselors, psychologists, and other mental health professionals, who work with the families of ADHD children, can use these approaches as well. They, too, can help to coordinate the efforts between home and school to increase the likelihood of the child's success.

While some mention is made on what teachers can do in the classroom, our main purpose in writing this book was to present a comprehensive combination of strategies that parents can use to help their ADHD child to do better at home, school, and in the community. As stressed previously, parents are the child's primary and most important teachers. And it is the parents of ADHD children and those professionals who work with them for whom this book is intended. Hopefully, the information that is presented will be a valuable source for helping to rear and educate these often misunderstood and challenging young people.

# INTRODUCTION

This book is about the rearing and education of children diagnosed with attention deficit hyperactivity disorder (ADHD). Children diagnosed with ADHD are at a high risk for failure. Because they are impulsive, inattentive and in constant counter-productive motion, their relationships with teachers, parents, and peers are frequently strained. Moreover, ADHD children often receive considerably more negative feedback than their normally functioning peers. This leads to strong feelings of hurt and frustration, a poor self-concept, and a lack of confidence in their ability to perform successfully. Without appropriate, comprehensive intervention, this cycle of social, emotional, and behavioral poverty only worsens with the passage of time. ADHD children have numerous problems, which if ignored and left untreated, can cause society considerable difficulty over the long run. The end result can and often does lead to anti-social behavior, low or nonexistent academic productivity, dropping out of school, and the development of a generally negativistic or surly attitude. The latter usually maligns their relationship not only with teachers, but potential employers and other persons in authority. It only makes sense, therefore, that early intervention programs that correctly diagnose and treat the ADHD child should be constructed and implemented as soon as possible.

The emphasis of this book is directed toward providing guidance to parents of children who range in age from two to twelve. It is during these years that habits are formed and parents have maximum influence on their youngster's development. Parents who use their knowledge effectively during these early child-rearing years are more likely to have a positive impact on their youngster's character formation. Such early preparation increases the likelihood that the child will be successful in the future. The purpose of this book, therefore, is to provide various approaches that can be applied with ADHD children in this age group.

It should be emphasized that parents of ADHD children are even more likely to need professional assistance than parents of so-called "normal" children. Because of their ADHD child's deviant and erratic behavior, these parents are frequently under considerable stress. They often feel frustrated and depressed and blame themselves for their youngster's problems.

Parents of ADHD children want their offspring to do well in school, at home, and in the community. However, they are often at a loss as to how to bring this about. It is not unusual for them to have received ill-conceived advice or to be blamed by those around them who have little or no understanding of what it is like to rear, nurture, and discipline an ADHD child on a daily basis. As educators and mental health professionals, we need to break this cycle of insensitivity. We need to try to extend ourselves to these parents by offering help that truly addresses the specific problems of their child.

As the preceding indicates, helping the ADHD child's parents to rear and educate their offspring is of the utmost importance. This, in essence, is the purpose of this book. First, it provides structured programs using behavioral and cognitive-restructuring principles that work specifically with ADHD children. Second, it shows how these can be applied in both the home and school so that a true partnership can be established and maintained. And third, it provides a viable structure which enables educators and parents to work together so that improved behavior, learning, and a better self-concept can be assured for the ADHD child in the future.

In order to achieve the preceding objectives, the application of behavioral principles is advocated. Behavior modification has clearly been shown to be one of the most effective treatment modalities for working with ADHD children (Barkley,1990; Gomez & Cole 1991; Lavin, 1989; Lavin, 1991; Lavin, 1997). The programs presented in this book are designed so that the ADHD child is reinforced for concentrating, thinking before acting (the antidote to impulsivity), and task completion. In conjunction with behavior modification, various cognitive-restructuring approaches in order to help the child to think more productively and to take greater responsibility for the consequences of his or her actions are presented (Lavin, 2002). This combination of behavior modification and cognitive-restructuring increases the likelihood that the ADHD youngster will learn to function more successfully at home and school.

8

It is important to note that our multi-faceted approach requires that the child's time schedule and behavioral expectations be structured and monitored consistently throughout the day. This makes it more likely that the ADHD youngster will acquire better work habits and develop the self-control which has eluded him or her in the past. Moreover, this can then lead to the development of an internal locus of control. In other words, the ADHD child will learn to make good choices and to take responsibility for his or her own behavior. These positive changes will replace the blaming, antagonistic encounters that once characterized many of the ADHD child's interaction with persons in authority.

Finally, we would like to stress that there is no shortcut to successfully rearing and educating ADHD children to be responsible, productive adults. The methods in this book take time and consistent application if they are to produce the desired results. Being the parent or teacher of an ADHD child is not easy. It demands commitment and effort. However, if parents, educators and mental health professionals cooperate and work diligently together, the likelihood of these youngsters developing into happy, successful persons will be increased. As those of us at Norbel School have observed, such a combined effort can lead to the ADHD child becoming a viable, coping and integrated adult despite his or her so-called "handicapping condition." This, in and of itself, can be a considerable source of pride and satisfaction for educators, parents, and mental health professionals who are dedicated to helping these challenging young people.

# I. ADHD SYMPTOMS AND DETERMINING THEIR CAUSE

## Diagnostic labels and symptoms

The diagnosis of attention deficit hyperactivity disorder (ADHD) is usually made by a psychiatrist, psychologist, family physician, pediatrician, a neurologist or a clinical social worker. Often this occurs after the child has entered school. The teacher may inform the parents that their child is behaving poorly in the classroom and on the playground. He or she may be inattentive, impulsive, and disruptive. With the parents' permission, the school will forward a checklist and/or a description of the child's behavior to the pediatrician. This information, in conjunction with a history of the child's development, is used to make the diagnosis.

Attention deficit hyperactivity disorder (ADHD) has been given a variety of names in the past. Hyperactivity, hyperkinesias, minimal brain damage, minimal brain dysfunction, and maturational lag are some of the terms associated with this disorder. More recently, the American Psychiatric Association used attention deficit hyperactivity disorder as the diagnostic label for hyperactive children (*Diagnostic and Statistical Manual of Mental Disorders, Fourth Edition*, 1994).

Whatever the diagnostic term, hyperactive youngsters engage in a number of behavioral deviations and excesses over a long period of time. Behavioral deviations are actions that are developmentally inappropriate for a youngster's given age level. For example, a twelve-year-old boy who constantly insists that he should be first and pushes other children out of the way to be first in line would be behaving atypically in comparison to other children of the same age. Behavioral excesses, in comparison, are of two types. First, hyperactive children overreact. This often occurs when the child faces even minimally frustrating or challenging situations. Instead of calmly trying to solve the problem or asking for help, the youngster lashes out against the person or object that he or she perceives as being the source of his or her frustration. The second behavioral excess is the continuation of an activity even though restraint or discontinuance would be appropriate. For example, although playtime is over, Sam keeps walking around the room making noises and fidgeting with objects on a shelf while everyone else is seated and working on a sedentary activity.

**Behavioral deviations**

Behavioral deviations, as indicated previously, are actions that are developmentally inappropriate for a given child's age level. The deviations can be categorized into the following five groups: (1) distractibility, inattention, and poor concentration; (2) disorganization; (3) impulsivity; (4) poor social skills and self-centeredness; and (5) the failure to plan ahead and a disregard for consequences. Each of these categories will be focused upon separately.

1. Distractibility, inattention, and poor concentration

These symptoms, which frequently occur in school, are readily apparent in the ADHD child. For example, the child fails to sustain effort in the completion of classroom assignments. Sometimes the child begins the work but then starts daydreaming, appearing to be off in space. He or she is frequently distracted by sights and sounds that are usually and easily ignored by others both in and outside of the classroom. For example, a bird chirping outside a window, a car honking a horn, or a child passing in the hall will temporarily command the youngster's attention. Whereas other children can disregard these, ADHD youngsters cannot block them out. Their attention flits from one thing to another. Often the child does not follow directions. The youngster may forget instructions and turn in schoolwork that is incomplete. The ADHD child cannot seem to stick to the task at hand. Even if the work is finished, it is usually messy and inaccurate.

2. Disorganization

The ADHD child is poorly organized. School materials are in constant disarray. Books, papers, and pencils are often misplaced or lost. His or her notebook is incomplete and contains crumpled, messy papers that are purposelessly jammed into the binder. Homework assignments are written everywhere except in the assignment notebook, and then they are often written incompletely or inaccurately. If the child does the homework, it gets lost between home and school. Sometimes the youngster even forgets to turn it in. Lost homework, books, or supplies may turn up several days later, often found in some inappropriate places such as under the bed, behind a door, or in some obscure corner of the house. The child never seems to know how or why this occurred.

## 3. Impulsivity

The impulsive child often blurts out a response before the teacher even has a chance to complete the question. Or he or she rushes into an assignment without reading the directions and then can't understand why the work is inaccurate. ADHD youngsters may constantly interrupt other people. It never dawns on them that the other person is talking. Rather, the child is in a big hurry to make sure that he or she is heard. The child, rushing down the hall, may inadvertently bump into people. He doesn't seem to be able to stop from acting quickly even though this irritates other people.

## 4. Poor social skills and self-centeredness

Unfortunately, ADHD children are often disliked by their peers. When playing games, they fail to follow the rules, push ahead of others, or they may actually change or interpret the rules to suit themselves. Sometimes they become overly aggressive in enforcing the rules to obtain an advantage. ADHD children may bully others to get their way. They do not take the rights or feelings of others into consideration. Their own desires and needs are of primary concern. Typically, ADHD children blame others when difficulties arise. They fail to acknowledge any responsibility for contributing to the problem. Rather, it is always caused by someone else. He or she is never at fault. Obviously, such a child has few, if any, friends.

5. Failure to plan ahead and a disregard for consequences

ADHD children sometimes engage in reckless, dangerous behavior. They do not think about the possible harm that they might inflict on themselves or others. For example, the child may jump from a high place onto a concrete surface. Or he may ride a skateboard over very rough terrain, oblivious to the possible injury that could result from this behavior. Even with warnings, he continues on as though nothing will happen. The ADHD child roughhouses with younger siblings, pets, or objects. He or she is oblivious to the fact that the behavior could be harmful or destructive. ADHD children seem to have no fear of strange people or possibly dangerous situations and act as if they were invincible.

**Behavioral excesses**

As described previously, behavioral excesses are the continuation of activities when restraint or discontinuance would be more appropriate. These excesses can be categorized into the following four groups: (1) constant physical motion; (2) constant shifting of activity; (3) excessive talking; and (4) emotional excesses. Each of these categories will be discussed separately.

1. Constant physical motion

ADHD children cannot sit for more than a few minutes. They run and jump when they should be walking. For example, Robert constantly pokes or pushes other children. He may get up from his chair and wander around the classroom while the other students are seated. Even when Robert is sitting, he constantly fidgets or plays with objects. Although he may be watching a TV show or video that interests him, his body is still in motion. Robert cannot seem to make himself stop moving.

2. Constant shifting of activity

Constant shifting of activity is similar to what was discussed in the section on distractibility. The ADHD child is frequently distracted by sights and sounds that have nothing to do with the task at hand. For example, Jim can be working on arithmetic problems but the noise from a pencil dropped on the floor causes him to look around. His interest constantly moves from one object to another, resting only for a brief second on each. The teacher is talking, but the various colors and shapes in the room and the movement of another student absorbs his attention as much as what the teacher is saying. This constant shifting of activity occurs repeatedly throughout the day. Jim may be reading a book. However, a mark or tear on the page would be of as much concern as the words he is reading. He is overly attuned to the sensations of his body. Even the rubbing of his clothes against his skin or minor itches become of major importance in competing for his overall attention.

## 3. Excessive talking

The ADHD child typically talks more than other children in the group. He or she continues to talk even when quiet is called for. For example, Sarah continues to talk repeatedly although the discussion has ended. The fact that others are not interested or annoyed with her makes no difference. She just talks louder or more rapidly to get their attention. Being called "motor mouth," or otherwise insulted or ignored, would deter most youngsters from continuing. However, this only seems to put fuel in the ADHD child's engine. He or she continues to push on without considering others.

## 4. Emotional excesses

ADHD children have a low frustration tolerance. When confronted with adversity or challenge, it is not unusual for them to have a tantrum or become extremely excited. They may break objects, slam doors, or kick holes in a wall. If spanked, they become more excitable, appearing to lose control. Unlike normal children, ADHD youngsters have great difficulty turning off their emotional motor. They become easily excited when playing active games with parents or peers. Although the other children can calm down when the activity has ended, ADHD children cannot stop. They continue to run, jump, poke, or push despite the fact that they are becoming annoying. Even when others plead with the child to calm down, the ADHD child seems oblivious to their requests.

## Determining the causes of hyperactivity

It is important to keep in mind that the ADHD child's behavioral symptoms manifest themselves consistently each day at home, in school, and in social situations. Although there may be variations of the behavior in different circumstances, the characteristics just described are common to all ADHD youngsters. Thus, there is a good deal of similarity between ADHD children.

Despite the similarity of symptoms, the causes for the ADHD child's behavior can vary. In other words, there are a number of factors that can cause ADHD children to behave the way that they do. For example, allergic reactions, diabetes, diseases, or actual damage to the brain can be responsible for deviant and excessive activity in children. In addition, parental separation, divorce, or arguing and fighting in the child's presence can also cause a youngster to become frustrated, anxious, and depressed. The child's preoccupation with his or her emotional concerns stemming from parental discord can lead to distractibility and over activity. Some children become overactive when they eat foods containing chemicals or additives. Exposure to certain dyes, perfumes, fragrances or other environmental irritants can also trigger excessive activity. Children reared in inadequate, chaotic, or disorganized homes might display ADHD symptoms. The parents have never taken the time and effort to train these youngsters to discipline and control themselves. Thus, when these children enter school, they lack the personal and social skills needed to be successful. They cannot concentrate or make themselves perform as expected because they were never trained to do so.

The point to keep in mind is that there may be one or several causes responsible for the manifestation of ADHD symptoms. In order to help the child, parents must try to identify each of these causes. In order to achieve this objective, a detailed evaluation must be conducted to identify physical, cognitive, social, and emotional factors that are responsible for the child's maladaptive behavior. Once these factors are determined, then parents can develop a program to help the child to acquire the self-control, persistence, and the confidence to be successful.

# II. MEDICATION AND THE
# ADHD CHILD

There are few issues related to educating the ADHD student as full of potential "landmines" as the question of medication. Certainly, it appears that everyone has an opinion about this issue. Often these opinions are not based on research evidence and the views that people hold can become politicized beyond the realm of reasonableness. The evidence shows that a combination of certain medications and a well-designed and implemented behavior modification program is the most effective approach to help children to cope with the symptoms associated with ADHD (National Institute of Mental Health, 1999 Publication; *The Multimodel Treatment Study of Children with Attention Deficit Hyperactivity Disorder*). And yet, many parents of children with ADHD are unaware of the importance of including the latter in their treatment regimen.

As indicted previously, the diagnosis of ADHD is usually made by a physician, a psychiatrist, a psychologist, a pediatrician, a neurologist or a clinical social worker. This often comes after months of frustration from the teacher, the parents, and the child. Psychological and educational testing usually follows months of notes, phone calls, and conferences highlighting the child's behavior and academic shortcomings. Once the preceding is completed, the diagnosis is presented and treatment options are discussed. Unfortunately, these are often presented as a picture of simplicity when, in fact, the dynamics influencing the child's behavior are quite complex.

Most often, the child's academic difficulty is overshadowed by behavior problems in the classroom. Dealing with such problems takes time away from the other children. When results are presented to parents, it is often the disruptive behavior and the inattentiveness that is sighted as the root of the child's academic difficulty. However, ADHD is actually quite complicated, and the child's poor behavior and inattentiveness are merely the outward manifestations of this complex problem. The general belief is that if these symptoms are "fixed" then the academic difficulties will be solved. Further, eliminating the child's behavioral problems is beneficial to the entire class.

**Why medication is an attractive solution**

Medication is an attractive solution for several reasons. First and foremost, medication can immediately improve the ADHD child's capacity to concentrate. Disruptive behavior often diminishes, and the child can become more manageable. Medication, therefore, can be presented as a "quick fix" for a difficult problem.

Quite naturally, parents fear that their child will fail academically. It is no wonder, therefore, that they perceive this as a most viable option for helping their child. However, this is not the only factor that makes medication such an attractive solution. Trust in professionals often influences their decision as well. Parents want to believe that physicians, teachers, and mental health specialists would only prescribe safe, effective treatments. As a result, they often fail to ask about the existence and viability of other methods for treating ADHD. Parents are told that medicine will calm the child and improve his or her academic performance, even though the evidence is quite mixed in this regard. Given such limited information, it makes sense that they might erroneously conclude that medication is both the best and only action to take.

Beside trust, the desire to be agreeable and cooperative can also make the decision to medicate an attractive one. Parents want to get along with their child's teacher. They are usually reluctant to challenge the school's opinion because they fear alienating themselves and their child. In fact, schools sometimes pressure parents to go along with their recommendations. They can insist that the distractible, disruptive behavior improve immediately. Suspensions, expulsions, or other punitive measures are sometimes threatened. Parents can sense when a teacher is becoming increasingly irritated with their ADHD child. This irritation may increase if they question the use of medication, which would actually make the teacher's job easier.

In summary, many parents agree to a regimen of medication without fully understanding the consequences of their choice. In fact, parents are often unaware that other treatments are available. They have simply been advised that medication is the best and only needed solution to their child's problem. They do not know that family counseling and behavior modification have been successful in helping ADHD youngsters. Further, many parents have little or no knowledge of the possible hazards or long-term consequences of taking medication. Instead, they believe that medication will improve their child's academic performance and enhance his or her self-esteem. Again, the evidence is quite mixed in this regard.

Naturally, many parents are concerned about the dangers that drugs might pose for their youngster, both now and in the future. Their concern is understandable. Medication is potentially physically and psychologically harmful. Medication does not necessarily improve academic performance; it does not build self-confidence; and it does not help the child to become responsible for his or her own behavior. In fact, many youngsters resist taking medication because they don't want to be different from their peers. They don't want to be perceived as being "crazy" because they have to take pills to control their behavior. Most children want to be successful using their own cognitive and emotional resources. However, they are often confused as to how to cope with their difficulties. Unfortunately, the parents of ADHD children may be equally bewildered. They may also be unaware that there are better and safer ways to help their youngsters to achieve successfully.

**Behavioral drugs and their hazards**

According to The National Institute of Mental Health (2003 revision of *Attention Deficit Disorder* by Margaret Strock), stimulants appear to be the most effective medications for treating ADHD. The following is a list of trade and generic names of each drug and the approved age for its administration:

| Trade Name | Generic Name | Approved Age |
|---|---|---|
| Adderall | Amphetamine | 3 and older |
| Concerta | Methylpenidate (long acting) | 6 and older |
| Cylert | Pemoline | 6 and older |
| Dexadrine | Dextroamphetamine | 3 and older |
| Dextrostat | Dextroamphetamine | 3 and older |
| Focaline | Dexmethylphenidate | 6 and older |
| Methadate ER | Methylphenidate (extended release) | 6 and older |
| Methadate CD | Methylphenidate (extended release) | 6 and older |
| Ritalin | Methylphenidate | 6 and older |
| Ritalin SR | Methylphenidate (extended release) | 6 and older |
| Ritalin LA | Methylphenidate (long acting) | 6 and older |

Because of its potential for causing serious liver function problems, Cylert should not be the first choice of medication in treating ADHD. Rather, it should be used only after the trial of several other stimulant drugs.

The most common side effects encountered with stimulant drugs are loss of appetite, weight loss, sleeping problems, irritability, restlessness, stomachache, headache, rapid heart rate, elevated blood pressure, and sudden behavior deterioration. Moreover, symptoms of depression involving sadness, crying, and withdrawal can occur. Two of the most disconcerting side effects are the intensification of tics, muscle twitches in the face and other parts of the body, and suppression of growth. While it is rare that a stimulant medication might cause tics, it could be responsible for activating and underlying tic condition. There is some concern that this could lead to a severe tic disorder called Gilles de la Tourette syndrome.

## The psychological pitfalls of medication

Another problem frequently occurring with children diagnosed with ADHD is low self-esteem. Often they feel powerless and inferior in comparison to their peers. In other words, ADHD children become depressed. They lack confidence in themselves. Putting a child on drugs may simply confirm that his or her behavior problems are caused by factors beyond his or her control. What message are we conveying to a child when we place him or her on drugs? Aren't we telling the youngster that he or she is incapable of learning self-control and achieving success using his or her own resources? Further, aren't we inadvertently increasing the likelihood that the child will fail to take responsibility for his or her own behavior? Medication makes it easier to attribute success and failure to a pill. If the child does well, it is the pill that enabled him or her to concentrate. If the child fails, it is because he or she "forgot" or refused to take the medication. Most parents want to rear self-confident children. Parents want their children to plan ahead and to take responsibility for their own behavior. Keeping this in mind, it doesn't make sense to only medicate children. It confirms that we believe that they lack the inner resources to control themselves and their environment. If a parent lacks confidence in a child, it is unlikely that the child will believe in him or herself. A child looks to the parents for verification of his or her ability. If the parents become discouraged, we can expect that the child will become discouraged as well. It is no wonder that ADHD children have such low self-esteem. Using medication as the only treatment takes away the opportunity for them to prove that they, and not the pill, can be successful.

Treating the ADHD child only with medication doesn't make sense for another reason. There is research indicating that successful, achieving children develop what is called an "internal locus of control" (Crandall, Katkovsky, & Crandall, 1965; Gagne, 1975; Seligman, 1975). This means that these youngsters believe that they are responsible for what happens to them. In other words, they believe that their successes and failures are caused by their own behavior. Successful children avoid making excuses. It is not external events such as luck, fate, or other people that enable them to do well in life. Rather, it is their initiative and efforts that lead to success. Again, putting a child only on medication is contrary to the notion of responsibility that parents want to instill in their children. Drug therapy without the inclusion of other treatment modalities suggests that the child has a "disease." Medication arrests the disease, enabling the child to concentrate better. The important point to remember is that drugs do not teach or train the child. Parents, teachers, and other adults are responsible for this. If we want responsible behavior and improved academic performance, it would make better sense to structure the environment to bring this about. Overactive youngsters can be trained to control themselves and to learn appropriate academic skills. In fact, there are a number of studies indicating that a high degree of environmental structure and consistent reinforcement produces such results. Thus, it makes sense to devise programs that teach and reinforce behavioral control rather than simply prescribe drugs as the cure-all for the problem.

There is another important point parents should consider before putting a child on a medication regimen. The 2000 edition of *The Physician's Desk Reference* states that if stimulant drugs are prescribed for ADHD children, they should be used as "an integral part of a total treatment program which includes other remedial measures (psychological, educational, social) for a stabilizing effect." This means that medication should not be the only means for helping the ADHD child. Psychological, educational, and social interventions should be used as well. Unfortunately, once a child is put on medication and it produces a calming effect, the drug may then become the total treatment program. The child may not receive sorely needed special educational services for his or her learning problems. It can easily be assumed that if the child is more behaviorally compliant, the other problems will simply take care of themselves. However, this is hardly the case. And this is why other combined behavioral and educational interventions are needed.

Finally, it should be stressed that *The Physician's Desk Reference* states that stimulant medication is not indicated for all children with ADHD symptoms. Children who "exhibit symptoms secondary to environmental factors" should not be medicated. In other words, children whose poor concentration and over-activity are caused by environmental factors (family dysfunction or a disorganized, chaotic home environment) should not be put on drugs. Rather, an appropriate educational placement and psychological treatment are recommended. Many times children are medicated when environmental stressors or lack of proper training are responsible for their problems. Divorce, separation, and marital and family discord are increasingly becoming more common in our society. It is no wonder that some of our children behave so poorly. Medicating the child is not the cure for inadequate parenting or poor teaching. However, it often becomes the crutch to lean on.

# III. APPLYING BEHAVIORAL PRINCIPLES WITH THE ADHD CHILD

## Goals of behavior modification

Research shows that behavior modification is one of the most effective modalities for working with the ADHD child (Barkley, 1990; Byrd & Byrd, 1986; Gomez & Cole, 1991; McGuiness, 1985; Lavin, 1991; Lavin, 1997). As noted earlier, research has shown that successful children believe that they succeed or fail because of the choices that they make. These young people have what is called an "internal locus of control" (Crandall, Katkovsky, & Crandall, 1965; Dweck, 1976; Gagne, 1975; Linn & Hodge, 1982; Rosenbaum & Baker, 1984; Seligman, 1975). Again, it should be stressed that successful children tend to take responsibility for their behavior. They do not believe that luck, outside events, or other people determine their success. As emphasized previously, most parents want their children to be productive and achievement oriented. They want their children to think ahead, to make good choices, and to take responsibility for their actions. Although medication calms ADHD children, it teaches none of these skills. Medication does not train children to control themselves, to be persistent, or to plan ahead. The proper application of behavior principles, on the other hand, can be used to teach ADHD children to acquire these skills.

One of the biggest complaints about ADHD children is that they are impulsive. Impulsivity is acting without forethought or planning. Because ADHD children frequently fail to think first and plan ahead, they often do poorly in school and have interpersonal problems with adults and peers. Thus, ADHD children must learn to direct, control, and monitor their energy if they are to be successful. Behavioral principles, when properly applied, do train ADHD children to concentrate and stay on task, to delay gratification, and to think ahead. A well-designed and implemented behavior modification program can help ADHD youngsters to learn that their actions, and not external factors, are responsible for success or failure. We believe that is the most effective way of assisting ADHD children in acquiring the skills and confidence needed to be productive in life.

## Teaching the child to accept responsibility

In order for an ADHD child, or any child, to learn to take responsibility, parents must begin by teaching the youngster that his or her behavior causes success or failure. The child must be taught two things: if he or she chooses to behave appropriately, positive consequences will follow; on the other hand, if he or she behaves inappropriately, negative consequences will follow. Parents usually begin to teach the latter when the child is very young. For example, Robert is taught that if he puts his hand on a hot stove, he will get burned. It is important for Robert to understand that putting his hand on the stove causes the pain to occur. In other words, his behavior, not the stove, is responsible for the burn. The message in this example is clear. Robert is taught that if he thinks before acting, unnecessary pain can be avoided. Parents can use these everyday situations to point out the cause and effect relationship of human behavior. This instruction serves as a bulwark against impulsivity. It provides the basis of good planning and self-control.

There are a number of other everyday occurrences that can be used to teach the child to control his or her impulsivity and to plan ahead. For example, a common problem that a mother experiences is the child interrupting or making demands when she is talking on the telephone. The mother who attends to the interruption or gives in to the child's demands is actually rewarding this obnoxious behavior. Thus, the child is more likely to do this again and again. In order to stop this behavior, the mother must state that interruptions and demands will not be tolerated. It they occur, the child will be sent to his or her room. Further, the youngster's requests will not be granted. Mother must specifically point out to the child that the interruptions and demands lead to punishment. They provide no chance of getting what the child wants. Again, in this example, we are teaching the child to curb impulsivity and to anticipate consequences. This is the basis upon which self-control is built.

Meals provide another opportunity for the parents to teach the child to plan ahead and to use good judgment. Consider the following: Sandra gets up in the morning and tells Mother that she wants Crispy, Crunchy Creatures for breakfast. Mom takes out the cereal, puts it into a bowl, and pours milk over it. Ten minutes later, Sandra is dawdling while eating the cereal. As a result, it becomes exceedingly mushy and very soggy. Sandra whines and complains that the cereal is unappetizing, and she refuses to eat it. Mother then makes her a pancake breakfast and Sandra stops the whining and complaining. What has Mother inadvertently taught Sandra? First, Sandra has learned to avoid her responsibility for choosing the cereal for breakfast. Second, she has learned that if she cries and complains long and loud enough, Mother will take away the unpleasantness that she has brought on herself. Thus, in this simple ordinary situation, the stage is set for teaching Sandra poor frustration control, avoidance of responsibility, and poor planning skills. If parents continue to indulge their youngster in this manner over a number of years, it will lead to the development of a "spoiled child." who will be unable to tolerate even minimal adversity.

The purpose of these examples is to emphasize that there are a number of daily situations parents can use to teach children to be responsible, successful persons. However, in order to instruct them effectively, basic principles must be kept in mind.

## General behavioral principles

There are a few general principles upon which all behavior modification programs are based. These are the foundation for training children to accept responsibility for their actions. First, as noted previously, there are situations which arise daily that parents can use to teach their child to plan ahead and to use good judgment. Second, parents must remember that what follows a behavior determines whether or not it will continue. Thus, it is of the utmost importance that the reward be given after behaving responsibly, not before. For instance, when parents want their child to eat vegetables, they should make a statement such as, "First eat the peas, and then you can have the ice cream." Most people recognize that if the child is allowed to eat the ice cream first, it is unlikely that the peas will ever be eaten. This is generally true for all activities that require hard work and effort. If the reward is given first, procrastination is likely to follow. This occurs because the motivation to work has been taken away. Common sense tells us that. For example, how often does a child complete homework satisfactorily if he or she starts it after watching TV or playing all day?

Another general principle to keep in mind is that in order to stop an undesirable behavior, unpleasant consequences must follow it. If a child behaves badly, and fails to get what he or she wants, then it is less likely that such behavior will occur in the future. If there is no payoff for inappropriate behavior, the child will eventually recognize that it makes no sense to continue acting in this way. Moreover, if unpleasant consequences such as a loss of privileges, isolation from the family, or restitution are attached to the behavior, the child is more likely to learn that the price to pay for acting badly is not worth it. Again, this increases the likelihood that inappropriate behavior will be discontinued.

## Behavioral principles specifically for the ADHD child

The application of behavioral principles with ADHD children has three goals in mind: to improve concentration, to encourage on task behavior; and to reduce impulsivity. These principles are as follows:

1.   The ADHD child's environment must be consistently structured from the time he or she gets up in the morning until bedtime. There should be little or no variation in behavioral requirements from one day to the next. Routines and repetition of "the same old behaviors" from one day to the next must be required. Once these become a habit, they can be replaced with new behaviors. Again, consistency, repetition, and persistence must be emphasized.

2.   Identify material objects and activities that can serve as rewards for complying with the system. All objects, activities, and privileges which the child finds to be desirable qualify as potential rewards for appropriate behavior. Keep in mind that you must distinguish between necessities and luxuries in forming this list. Necessities are objects and activities that are essential to the child's education, health, or general well being. Luxuries, on the other hand, would be items and activities such as

junk foods, sodas, TV, computer games, bicycle riding, pleasure reading, going to the movies, or trips to recreational facilities. Necessities are materials for school, nutritional foods (not necessarily pleasant tasting), appropriate clothing (not "brand-name" items; these can be earned), and medical attention. Make sure that all potential rewards, therefore, are no longer given without earning them. In other words, there is no more "free lunch." As one rebellious young man complained to us, "I have to buy my life." There was some truth to his complaint. However, once he gave up the "power struggle" and cooperated with the system, he admitted that the progress that he made was worth it. In fact, when given the opportunity to discontinue the program, he chose to keep it in force.

3.    Identify all inappropriate behaviors and the penalties that can be applied to them. The failure to behave responsibly must be stopped and replaced with desirable behavior. Be prepared to give a "hefty fine" or to apply an intensely negative consequence when inappropriate behavior occurs. Make sure to identify penalties and losses of privilege that will be missed by your ADHD child. Don't be discouraged when the child says, "I don't care." Even though the loss may be painful, he or she is not likely to admit this. In fact, his or her appearance may be quite the opposite of one who is disappointed. The loss will hurt, but the child will be darned if he or she shows this.

4.    When punishing the ADHD child, there are certain principles which must be kept in mind. First, the punishment for inappropriate behavior should be immediate. Do not wait. The punishment should be as closely associated with the behavior as possible. Because ADHD children are easily distracted and have concentration problems, this close association increases the likelihood that they will learn from their mistake. Again, the goal is to make sure that the child connects the infraction with the consequence. The immediate punishment of deviant behavior makes it more likely that this will occur.

Second, because the ADHD child can be annoying, particularly to those adults who work with him or her on a daily basis, it is important to remain dispassionate in applying the punishment. Provide a short explanation on why punishment is being given. Avoid getting into a heated debate. It is most important to avoid getting into a meaningless power struggle. This only rewards arguing, which is one of the behaviors that you are trying to eliminate.

Third, because the ADHD child frequently complains that "life is unfair" and that "everyone is out to get them," try to convey to him or her that you are sorry that you have to administer the punishment. Let the child know that you care about him or her and that you want him or her to be successful. In other words, be supportive in conjunction with your firm, no-nonsense attitude. This will help to diffuse the ADHD youngster's negativism and makes it less likely that a "power struggle" will occur. The less defensive the child becomes, the greater the possibility that he or she will learn from mistakes.

5.  In setting up any behavioral program, it is important to begin by rewarding the successful completion of easy tasks first. You may then move to the rewarding of more difficult tasks later on. Quick beginning success makes it more likely that the child will "get hooked" into the program. Once this occurs, more difficult tasks can be added to the daily and weekly agenda.

6.  Because the ADHD child is distractible, it is important to keep competing stimuli from interfering with his or her concentration. In other words, when trying to get the child to focus on a specific task, distracting sounds and sights must be eliminated. This increases the likelihood that the youngster will pay attention to what is required.

7.  Because ADHD children can be quite demanding, it is important for parents to be equally persistent in holding their child accountable for his or her behavior. In other words, "stick to your guns" no matter how pleading or obnoxious the child becomes. If you give in to unreasonable demands, you will inadvertently be rewarding the very behavior that you are trying to eliminate. By holding firm, however, you will be forcing the child to look for more viable alternatives to obtain the attention and rewards that he or she is seeking.

8.  Make sure that good self-control and responsible choice making are recognized and praised. Identify what the child did to demonstrate these and follow them with a compliment. This makes it more likely that the child will view you in a positive light and want to please you. Moreover, it increases the possibility that the child will work "for the right reasons" rather than the material rewards which follow appropriate behavior.

9.  Both parents must agree on the required behaviors and how the program is to be implemented. They must consistently follow through so

that the child is not allowed to deviate from the requirements or to "play one parent off against the other." The program will be sabotaged if the preceding is allowed to occur. Parents will then spend more time fighting with each other than modifying the child's behavior. ADHD children have a knack for manipulating parents. This must be curbed so that the program's effectiveness does not get undermined.

10. Before the program is put into effect, make sure that the child fully understands the expected requirements. Remember that the ADHD child is distractible, forgets quickly, and often fails to attend to the task at hand. Therefore, after you have explained the behavioral expectations, have the youngster repeat these back to you. Make sure that this is done completely and accurately. If the child's explanation is confusing or incomplete, go back over the requirements until he or she "gets it." In fact, it is a good idea to reward the youngster for successfully describing the requirements of the program. This reinforces concentration, which is a skill that you want your child to acquire. Having the child actually demonstrate the required activity can also be very helpful. Keep in mind that repetition and "over-learning" are likely to insure that the ADHD child will remember to follow through on the required tasks. This is how he or she learns to develop good habits.

11. If one of the parents is largely responsible for rearing the ADHD child, that parent will need relief from time to time. Periodic "rest and relaxation" is necessary because the daily challenge of coping with an ADHD child can be an emotionally draining, frustrating, and discouraging task. This can lead to "burn out" and even despair. All of us need to have our batteries periodically "recharged." This is particularly important for parents of ADHD children. Arrangements need to be made for the less involved parent to take over so that the more involved parent can "escape" once in awhile. If both parents are equally involved, grandparents, friends, or other supportive people might be asked for assistance from time to time. If parents are members of a support group that is concerned with the rearing and education of ADHD children, they may be able to arrange a trade in which they exchange supervision responsibilities with other interested members. Again, it is important to stress that being a parent of an ADHD child is difficult, time consuming, and very challenging. Unless parents manage their time, energy, and resources wisely, it is easy to become overwhelmed and discouraged.

12. Communicate clearly, concretely, and behaviorally with the ADHD child. Tell him or her in behavioral terms what is expected. For example, say, "Sit upright in your chair; keep both feet flat on the floor; and eat with your fork" rather than "Be good at the table." Ambiguity will come back to haunt you in the form of whining, rebellious statements such as, "I was being good. You're just mean."

13. The ADHD child is easily excited. He or she has much difficulty remaining calm and controlling his or her emotions. Thus, it is important for parents to try to be as emotionally low-keyed as possible. Since the ADHD child loses control easily, parents must try to remain calm. Avoid condemnations such as, "You're a bad boy (or girl)." Curb behavior early before it gets out of hand. Parents should specifically comment on the behavior and request that it come under immediate control. If this does not occur, the child should be removed to an isolated location until he or she becomes calm again.

14. ADHD children do not easily transition from one situation to another. For example, going from a well-structured home environment to a family reunion, a grocery store, or a birthday party with other children can trigger considerable excitement and "out of control" behavior. It is important, therefore, to discuss these transitions in advance; the behavioral expectations before, during, and while the child is there; and the immediate consequences that will apply should inappropriate behavior occur. Rewards for good behavior and penalties for rule violations should be established in advance. Also, parents should be prepared to remove the child from the situation and to immediately return home should infractions occur. Again, this all should be discussed in advance with the child so that he or she will be mentally prepared for coping with the anticipated event.

15. The ADHD child becomes frustrated easily. Thus, it is important to reward the youngster when he or she demonstrates good self-control. When the child is disappointed or is having difficulty but does not lose his or her temper, parents should comment on this. Specifically, the child should be told that he or she is showing good self-control. Praising self-control is rewarding to the ADHD child.

16. Because the ADHD child loses his or her temper quickly, teaching the youngster to maintain control is helpful. When the child is frustrated, he or she can be instructed to take a deep breath and count to

ten. The youngster can then say the words, "be calm." When the child gains control, he or she can talk with the parents about the problem. They can then suggest various approaches for appropriately coping with frustration.

17.  Because ADHD children have such difficulty with concentration, memory, and self-control, inventing games to practice in improving these skills can be helpful. For example, parents can have the child sit in a chair without moving his or her hands, legs, or head for a specified period of time. Or the child might be asked to carry out silly instructions such as, "take a book from the shelf with your left hand and kneel on it with your right knee." If the child performs these exercises successfully, a reward can be given to him or her. Such games train the child in both body control and listening. More on self-control games will be presented in a later chapter.

18.  Each evening, parents should have a family meeting with their child. They should discuss the activities that the child has performed successfully and unsuccessfully for that day. At the end of the meeting, the youngster should be asked to repeat the material that was discussed. This indicates to the parents that he or she is listening and understands what they are saying. If the child makes mistakes or omits information in the summary, parents should make the necessary corrections. The child is then asked to review the behaviors again. It is important to keep in mind that repetition will enhance the ADHD child's concentration and memory. This makes it more likely that he or she will retain the information conveyed to him or her.

## Summary on application of behavior principles

The ADHD child has special problems which interfere with his or her ability to function successfully at home and school. He or she is distractible, inattentive, and impulsive. These characteristics must be taken into account in planning a behavioral program. Because the ADHD child is so easily distracted, it is important for parents to require that their child attend to what they are saying. They must make sure that the youngster makes eye contact and acts as though he or she was seriously listening to them. Having the child repeat instructions helps him or her to retain information. It also enables the parents to be sure that the youngster understands their expectations.

As emphasized previously, one of the biggest problems for the ADHD child is impulsivity. Parents can train the child to be less impulsive and to gain greater self-control if they actively praise and reward this. In addition, parents can teach the child to think before he or she acts by using simple games and exercises.

Finally, parental consistency is very important in dealing with the ADHD child. Parents must agree on expected behaviors and appropriate rewards and penalties. They must remain firm but emotionally low-keyed because the ADHD child becomes easily excited. Further, the ADHD child often becomes discouraged and gives up easily. He or she lacks confidence. Therefore, it is important for parents to be encouraging and to provide experiences that will enable the child to achieve successfully. Such success will help the youngster to believe that he or she has the ability to overcome adversity and the many challenges of everyday living.

In summary, any program that is developed in working with ADHD children should be designed so that they are required to concentrate, stay on task, plan ahead, and engage in goal directed activity. These behaviors then replace the inattentiveness, impulsivity, and misdirected activity which is so characteristic of ADHD children. Parents who effectively plan and implement a good behavior modification program are teaching their children to make good choices and to assume responsibility for their actions. Further, by training their children to behave appropriately, they are helping their youngsters to develop confidence, improve their coping skills, and perform successfully at home and school. Putting the preceding into practice is not easy, however. Parents must be consistent, firm, and hold the child accountable. They must work together, present a "united front," and be persistent in requiring the child to behave responsibly. Parents need to be committed to the use of behavioral principles. They must recognize that if they "stick to their guns," they can turn their ADHD child in a positive direction. While this is a challenging task, it can be done, provided that they stay committed over "the long haul." Remaining positive in the face of adversity is a key component to parenting successfully. This is particularly necessary with youngsters who are unfortunately afflicted with attention deficit hyperactivity disorder.

# IV. DEVELOPING A BEHAVIOR MODIFICATION PLAN AT HOME

As indicated in the previous chapter, any behavior modification program which is used with the ADHD child should teach him or her to concentrate, stay on task, plan ahead, and engage in goal directed activity. The program should require skills which negate or are contrary to ADHD characteristics. Moreover, any good behavior program should teach the child to make responsible choices and to delay gratification. This is particularly important in curbing impulsivity and acquiring self-control.

The first step in teaching the child to make good choices is motivating him or her to do so. This can be accomplished by rewarding or paying points to the youngster when he or she chooses to behave appropriately. The points can then be used to immediately purchase desirable rewards. Delay of gratification, on the other hand, can be taught by motivating the child to save rather than spend the points. The accumulated points can eventually be used to purchase rewards of greater value. This teaches the child that persistence and sustained goal directed effort over an extended period of time can lead to far greater rewards in the future. In this way, the child learns to delay gratification, which is particularly important to later success in life. For example, young people who choose to go to college give up immediate financial benefits and independence by becoming employed. However, once they complete their education, they usually make more money over their lifetime than those who choose not to go to college. Thus, programs which motivate the child to think and to plan ahead teach him or her to delay gratification. This is the antithesis of impulsivity, which is one of the major obstacles that the ADHD child must overcome.

## Identifying and Classifying Positive and Negative Behaviors

With the preceding in mind, the first step is to formulate a plan to achieve these objectives. This can be accomplished by devising a home-based system that rewards responsible behavior and penalizes behavior that is irresponsible. We need to begin by identifying those specific behaviors that we want the child to perform consistently each day. Once these have been determined, they should be divided into three groups— morning, afternoon, and evening behaviors. The order of their occurrences may be as follows:

### Morning Behaviors
1. Ready for school by 8 a.m.
2. Eat breakfast properly
3. Brush teeth
4. At the bus by 8:45

### Afternoon Behaviors
1. Bring home daily school report
2. Bring home school materials
3. Homework completed accurately
4. Pack school materials for next day

### Evening
1. Eat supper properly
2. Take bath or shower
3. Brush teeth
4. In bed by 9 p.m.

The reader will note that these tasks are arranged in a chronological time sequence encompassing the entire day. Some of the tasks are relatively easy, whereas others are much more difficult. Moreover, the afternoon behaviors focus mainly on school related activities. Because parents are largely concerned with improving their ADHD child's academic performance, these behaviors must have a prominent place in the program. They, therefore, need to be emphasized and rewarded accordingly. In fact, parents may want to include a behavioral category entitled "Good Day at School." If the child performs well that day (as determined from a daily school report), he or she would receive extra points. The details for implementing this will be discussed in the next chapter.

It should be noted that the school related behaviors are all required in the afternoon, right after school. The program is arranged in this way because this is the best time to complete these tasks. If these are allowed to "drag on" or to occur in the evening hours, the chances are good that they will be done poorly or not at all. Once these activities have been completed satisfactorily, then the rest of the day can be enjoyed without the anticipated pressure of trying to complete these when everyone is tired and "had it" by the end of the evening. Also, once the school work is done, it makes it more likely that the day can end on a pleasant note. This puts everyone in a more positive frame of mind as they prepare for the next day when the routine begins again.

Once the morning, afternoon, and evening behaviors have been designated and chronologically arranged, the next step is to identify those behaviors that are inappropriate and must be penalized. A sample of some inappropriate behaviors is as follows:

1.  Failure to bring home daily school report
2.  Failure to bring home needed school materials
3.  Disobedience
4.  Lying
5.  Loss of temper, cussing
6.  Back talk

Again, the reader will note the emphasis on school related tasks with samples one and two. By penalizing the child's "failures" (samples one and two) and rewarding good school performance, parents are not only facilitating home-school cooperation but they make it more likely that their ADHD child will learn as expected. This kind of comprehensive and thorough structure virtually insures that the child will be closely monitored and held accountable for almost all important school related activities.

**Identifying and Organizing the Reward System**

Once the positive and negative behaviors have been determined, the next step is to identify the various rewards that would serve as incentives to motivate the child. Keep in mind that all luxury items and privileges must now be earned. No longer are these given for free. As noted previously, the child is always provided with the necessities for his well-being. Television, videos, snack foods, movies, trips to a restaurant of his choice, amusements, and other "extras" must now be paid for out of the behavior modification system. A list of sample rewards that can serve as potential motivators are as follows:

1. Use of TV
2. Use of stereo
3. Video game time
4. Snacks, such as chips
5. Coke or other soft drink
6. Ride bike
7. Use of telephone
8. Stay up half hour later
9. Watch TV special
10. Go to library
11. Play game with a parent
12. Have parent read a story
13. Take a walk with parent
14. Have a friend over to play
15. Have a special dessert
16. Help Mom make dinner
17. Visit a friend
18. Draw, paint or make crafts
19. Read to a parent
20. Go to a fast food restaurant
21. Go to an expensive restaurant
22. Go out for ice cream
23. Rent a movie of choice
24. Have a friend overnight
25. Go to a friend's house overnight
26. Out for pizza
27. Order special meal at home
28. Movie
29. Ice skating
30. Go to movie
31. Buy a $5 toy
32. Fishing
33. Attend athletic event
34. Go to amusement park
35. Picnic at park
36. Visit grandparents
37. Go camping
38. Buy clothes
39. Go swimming
40. Take friend to restaurant or movie
41. Stay up late on the weekend
42. Go to the arcade
43. Buy a video game
44. Take a day trip of choice
45. Buy a CD
46. Use the computer

Once all of the potential rewards have been identified, the next step is to arrange them into categories: those which can be purchased daily and those which can be purchased by saving points over a long period of time. The purpose of having separated lists is two fold. First, the daily rewards will provide the child with those immediate incentives that are likely to "prime the pump," so to speak. In other words, these make the system immediately attractive to the child and encourage good performance right away. The long-term rewards, on the other hand, will require the child to save points to purchase them. This involves the delay of gratification, more thinking and planning ahead, greater concentration, and persistent on task behavior. Again, these are the very qualities that are contrary to ADHD characteristics and lead to higher levels of achievement and better self-control.

Daily rewards usually do not require that parents exert extra effort or expense. Long-term rewards, on the other hand, are the opposite of this. They can require a much longer time commitment, more effort, and can be far more costly. Thus, the child will have to be goal-directed and persistent in order to obtain such rewards. Some examples of "short-term" and "long-term" rewards are as follows:

| Short-term rewards | Long-term rewards |
|---|---|
| TV by half hour | Fast food outing |
| Video game by half hour | Expensive restaurant outing |
| Snacks | Amusement park |
| Play game with parent | Camping |
| Stay up fifteen minutes late | Trip to movies |
| Use of telephone (10 minutes) | Purchase a CD |
| Ride bike | Attend a special event (ballgame, etc.) |
| Friend over to play | Have a friend sleepover |

Once the preceding is completed, the positive behaviors, negative behaviors and daily rewards can be organized into a chart as shown on the next page. The reader will note that there are no long-term rewards listed on this chart. The reason for this is two fold: 1) The chart is organized and administered on a weekly basis and; 2) The long-term rewards are so expensive that ordinarily the child would not be able to accrue enough points in a week to purchase them. Rather, the child must save points if the more desirable long-term reward is to be earned. At the end of the week, these "saved" or surplus points can be transferred into a bank account through a certificate of deposit. The certificate of deposit is as follows:

Figure 1A: Sample CERTIFICATE OF DEPOSIT

| CERTIFICATE OF DEPOSIT | | | |
|---|---|---|---|
| Reward _____ | | | |
| Point Cost _____ | | | |
| Date of Deposit | Amount | Balance Due | Date of Purchase |
| | | | |
| | | | |
| | | | |

The certificate of deposit provides blank spaces in which the particular reward and point cost can be recorded. Rows and columns are provided in order to specify when the deposit is made, how much, the balance due and the final date of purchase. Once the child puts his or her points into the bank through a certificate of deposit, it cannot be taken out.

Each new week starts out with zero points on the behavior chart. Should the youngster falter and not have enough points for rewards on the new week, he or she cannot withdraw points from the bank to make up for the difference. All purchases must be made from the points accrued from the new week alone. This makes it more likely that the child will not take a vacation from the system and rely on past performance to get what he or she wants. Rather, the youngster will have to maintain consistent, goal-directed behavior every week to be rewarded accordingly.

**Organizing a behavioral chart**

As noted previously, once the behaviors and daily rewards have been determined, the next step would be to arrange these on a chart using the following format:

## Figure 2A: Sample BEHAVIOR CHART

| Name _____ Start Date _____ End Date _____ | | | | | | | | | |
|---|---|---|---|---|---|---|---|---|---|
| **POSITIVE BEHAVIORS "P"** | | | | | | | | | |
| **Morning "P"** | Points | M | TU | W | TH | F | SA | SU. | Weekly Total |
| 1. | | | | | | | | | |
| 2. | | | | | | | | | |
| 3. | | | | | | | | | |
| 4. | | | | | | | | | |
| **Afternoon "P"** | X | X | X | X | X | X | X | X | X |
| 1. | | | | | | | | | |
| 2. | | | | | | | | | |
| 3. | | | | | | | | | |
| 4. | | | | | | | | | |
| **Evening "P"** | X | X | X | X | X | X | X | X | X |
| 1. | | | | | | | | | |
| 2. | | | | | | | | | |
| 3. | | | | | | | | | |
| 4. | | | | | | | | | |
| **Daily Total "P"** | X | | | | | | | | |
| **NEGATIVE BEHAVIORS "N"** | | | | | | | | | |
| 1. | | | | | | | | | |
| 2. | | | | | | | | | |
| 3. | | | | | | | | | |
| 4. | | | | | | | | | |
| **Daily Total "N"** | X | | | | | | | | |
| **DAILY REWARDS COST "C"** | | | | | | | | | |
| 1. | | | | | | | | | |
| 2. | | | | | | | | | |
| 3. | | | | | | | | | |
| 4. | | | | | | | | | |
| 5. | | | | | | | | | |
| 6. | | | | | | | | | |
| 7. | | | | | | | | | |
| 8. | | | | | | | | | |
| **Cost Total "C"** | X | | | | | | | | |
| **P-N-C =** | X | | | | | | | | |

In setting up the chart, the reader will note that the child's name and starting and ending dates for the week are placed at the top. The dates provide parents with an ongoing record so that they can assess the child's progress and make needed adjustments.

Further examination shows that Positive Behaviors "P," Negative Behaviors "N," and Daily Rewards are listed. The number of points that can be earned for Positive Behaviors "P" (Morning "P" + Afternoon "P" + Evening "P") and lost for Negative Behaviors "N" are presented in the points column. The Cost "C" of each daily reward is provided in the points column as well.

The chart is arranged in rows and columns so that the points gained, lost, and spent can be recorded for each day of the week. In this way, consistent and close monitoring of the child's behavior can be achieved. How the number of points is determined for each category will be discussed later. At this juncture, it is important to gain an overall sense of what the categories entail and how they function in providing consistent consequences for modifying the child's behavior.

The reader will note that there are three columns on the chart which are labeled as Daily Total "P," Daily Total "N," and Cost Total "C." Daily Total "P" is the sum of all the points earned for a particular day. Daily Total "N" is the opposite of this. It is the sum of those points lost for all behavior violations.

In order to determine whether the child can purchase daily rewards, the Daily Total "N" is subtracted from the Daily Total "P." If the latter is higher than the former, than the child will have points for purchasing rewards. However, if the reverse occurs, the child will be "in the red." He or she will, therefore, be unable to buy any rewards for that day. In other words, the youngster must be "in the black" in order to be able to buy the privileges on the chart.

The Cost Total "C" column is the sum of points that the child spends for all the rewards for that day. This Cost Total "C" is subtracted from those "in the black" points. This final tally is then recorded in the P-N-C Total. If there are any points left over, they are carried into the next day.

Lastly, it should be noted that, a Weekly Total column is provided following the days of the week. This is used to tabulate the total number of points that the child is spending for that week on various items and privileges. In this way, parents can keep tabs on those rewards that have the most appeal to their child. They may then want to increase the cost of some rewards and lower the cost of others in order to make the child expend more effort and to make better choices. For example, if the youngster is choosing TV most of the time, parents may want to increase the cost. The child will then have to earn and spend more points to watch TV. Below you will find a completed weekly BEHAVIOR CHART illustrating how the system operates.

Figure 3A: Completed Weekly BEHAVIOR CHART


See following page.


In examining the chart, the reader will note that Johnny can earn a maximum of 55 points a day for POSITIVE BEHAVIORS (Total of Morning, Afternoon, and Evening "P"). The number of points that can be taken away for NEGATIVE BEHAVIORS will vary according to the type and frequency of each rule violation. The number of points paid for DAILY REWARDS will also vary depending on the value of each reward. When a reward is purchased, it is subtracted from the surplus points that have been accumulated for that day.

In order to more fully understand how the system works, let's look at Johnny's BEHAVIOR CHART for Monday. Johnny earned all 55 points for positive behavior on that day. Unfortunately, however, he was penalized twice for back talking, which cost him 20 points. The 20 point violation was subtracted from the 55 points, thereby leaving him with 35 points left over. These points could be spent for a reward of his choosing. Johnny chose to watch a half hour of television, which cost him ten points. The ten points were then subtracted from the thirty-five points (P-C-N Total), leaving a remainder of twenty-five points for Monday. The twenty-five points would then be carried into the next day. Thus, Johnny would begin Tuesday with a twenty five-point debit which could be used to purchase more rewards.

| Name Johnny Smith | | | | Start Date 5-18-03 | | | End Date 5-25-03 | | |
|---|---|---|---|---|---|---|---|---|---|
| **POSITIVE BEHAVIORS "P"** | | | | | | | | | |
| **Morning "P"** | Points | M | TU | W | TH. | F. | SA | SU | Weekly Total |
| 1.Ready for school 8.00 A.M. | 4 | 4 | 4 | 4 | 4 | 4 | 0 | 0 | 20 |
| 2 Eat breakfast | 4 | 4 | 4 | 4 | 4 | 4 | 4 | 4 | 28 |
| 3.Brush teeth | 3 | 3 | 3 | 3 | 3 | 3 | 3 | 3 | 21 |
| 4 Bus by 8 45 A.M. | 4 | 4 | 4 | 4 | 4 | 4 | 0 | 0 | 20 |
| **Afternoon "P"** | X | X | X | X | X | X | X | X | X |
| 1.Bring home daily school report | 5 | 5 | 5 | 5 | 5 | 5 | 0 | 0 | 25 |
| 2.Bring home required school materials | 5 | 5 | 5 | 5 | 5 | 5 | 0 | 0 | 25 |
| 3.Homework done neatly and accurately | 10 | 10 | 10 | 10 | 10 | 10 | 0 | 0 | 50 |
| 4.School materials packed for next day | 5 | 5 | 5 | 5 | 5 | 5 | 0 | 0 | 25 |
| **Evening "P"** | X | X | X | X | X | X | X | X | X |
| 1.Eat supper | 4 | 4 | 4 | 4 | 4 | 4 | 4 | 4 | 28 |
| 2.Take bath | 3 | 3 | 3 | 3 | 3 | 3 | 3 | 3 | 21 |
| 3.Brush teeth | 3 | 3 | 3 | 3 | 3 | 3 | 3 | 3 | 21 |
| 4.In bed by 9:00 P.M. | 5 | 5 | 5 | 5 | 5 | 5 | 5 | 5 | 35 |
| **Daily Total "P"** | X | 55 | 80 | 85 | 90 | 85 | 87 | 74 | 319 |
| **NEGATIVE BEHAVIORS "N"** | | | | | | | | | |
| 1.Failure to bring home school report | 25 | 0 | 0 | 0 | 0 | 0 | 0 | 0 | 0 |
| 2.Failure to bring home school materials | 25 | 0 | 0 | 0 | 0 | 0 | 0 | 0 | 0 |
| 3 Disobedience | 15 | 0 | 0 | 0 | 15 | 0 | 0 | 0 | 15 |
| 4.Arguing | 10 | 20 | 10 | 0 | 0 | 0 | 0 | 0 | 30 |
| **Daily Total "N"** | X | 20 | 10 | 0 | 15 | 0 | 0 | 0 | 45 |
| **DAILY REWARDS COST "C"** | | | | | | | | | |
| 1.T.V. by the half hour | 10 | 10 | 10 | 20 | 0 | 0 | 20 | 30 | 90 |
| 2.Video game by the half hour | 10 | 0 | 0 | 10 | 0 | 10 | 0 | 10 | 30 |
| 3.Snacks | 15 | 0 | 0 | 0 | 15 | 0 | 15 | 0 | 30 |
| 4.Play game with parent | 20 | 0 | 0 | 0 | 0 | 0 | 0 | 0 | 0 |
| 5.Soda | 10 | 0 | 10 | 10 | 10 | 0 | 0 | 0 | 30 |
| 6.Ride bike by half hour | 10 | 0 | 10 | 0 | 0 | 0 | 0 | 0 | 10 |
| 7.Friend over to play | 10 | 0 | 0 | 0 | 0 | 10 | 0 | 0 | 10 |
| 8.Stay up past bedtime fifteen minutes | 10 | 0 | 10 | 10 | 20 | 0 | 0 | 20 | 60 |
| **Cost Total "C"** | X | 10 | 40 | 50 | 45 | 20 | 35 | 60 | 260 |
| **P-N-C =** | X | 25 | 30 | 35 | 30 | 65 | 52 | 14 | 14 |

As indicated previously, this could work in reverse. Johnny's "P"–"N" Total could be "in the red." He could conceivably owe points because his negative points exceeded the positive behavior points. Should this occur, then Johnny would be unable to purchase any rewards. The reader should keep in mind that this is a "pay as you go" or "cash and carry" system. No rewards can be purchased on credit. If the child does not have the required number of points, no matter how much pleading or promising to pay later, the rewards are not given. It is this type of firmness, structure, and accountability that ultimately teaches and sustains good habits.

## Assigning points and implementing the program

As the preceding indicates, the earning and spending of points is the motivational foundation on which the home behavioral system is based. The ADHD child earns points for behaving responsibly and loses points for infractions. The child spends points to obtain all tangible items and privileges that serve as rewards for good behavior. Again, there is "no free lunch" in this program. It is a "pay as you go" system, requiring that appropriate behavior occurs before any payment of points is given.

In the previous sample, the reader will note that the points assigned to the easier tasks (e.g. Brush teeth, 3 points) were less than those assigned to the more difficult tasks (e.g. Homework done neatly and accurately, 10 points). This is the principle that determines how many points are given for each behavior. The more difficult the behavior, the more points that are assigned and vice versa. The same principle applies in assigning points to the various rewards. The immediate, lower level rewards can be purchased with fewer points than the more valuable, pleasurable, and satisfying rewards. The latter requires that the child save points, plan ahead, delay gratification, and persist in behaving appropriately. Again, these are character traits that ultimately lead to future success.

In determining the number of points that the ADHD child can earn for the week, two factors must be taken into consideration. First, the weekly total must be high enough so that immediate rewards can be purchased each day, provided that the child behaves appropriately. In other words, if the child has a good day, he or she should be able to earn enough points so that TV, snacks, and other immediate daily rewards can be purchased.

Second, the weekly point total should be low enough so that long-term "certificates of deposit" can only be purchased if the child saves points by not spending them on daily rewards. In other words, the child must decide that he or she would prefer to give up watching TV or purchasing snacks and save these points. These then could be credited toward the purchase of more valuable rewards like going to a favorite restaurant or movie, which is far more expensive than any of the short-term rewards.

In applying this to Johnny's weekly BEHAVIOR CHART, the reader will note that he had a good week at home and in school, earning a total of 319 points for POSITIVE BEHAVIORS. Johnny lost a total of 45 points for NEGATIVE BEHAVIORS and he spent 260 points for DAILY REWARDS. At the end of the week (5/25/03), Johnny had 14 points left over. He decided to purchase a CERTIFICATE OF DEPOSIT through the bank. His CERTIFICATE OF DEPOSIT was credited with an amount of 14 points towards the purchase of a pizza at his favorite restaurant. The cost for this long-term reward was 400 points. Thus, the balance due is 386 points. When this balance is paid, the date of purchase will be recorded on the CERTIFICATE OF DEPOSIT and Johnny will receive his reward.

As indicated earlier, CERTIFICATE OF DEPOSIT points cannot be withdrawn but must remain in the bank until the long-term reward is actually purchased. Some other long-term rewards that Johnny might have purchased and their suggested prices are as follows: 1) Fast food restaurant visit – 300 points; 2) Expensive restaurant visit – 600 points; 3) Friend overnight – 250 points; 4) Go to friend's overnight – 250 points; 5) Out for pizza – 400 points; 6) Order special meal at home – 200 points; 7) Rollerblading at park – 400 points; 8) Buy CD or video game – 750 points; 9) Movie – 300 points; 10) Rent a movie – 175 points; 11) Buy a ten dollar toy – 500 points; 12) Fishing – 600 points; 13) Ballgame – 500 points; 14) Amusement park 1,000 points or 15) Camping – 750 points.

In administering the program, it is important to provide the ADHD child with the opportunity to recover if he or she has had a bad week. Therefore, if the youngster is "in the red," owing points at the end of the week, it would be best to begin the next week starting at a zero level. There is no sense in "beating a dead horse" so to speak. If the child is doing poorly, then the system may need to be readjusted. Some point charges may need to be lowered and more encouragement to try to do better may be needed. Continuing to heap more punishment on the ADHD child is unlikely to motivate him or her. Rather, discouragement, hopelessness, and "an attitude" are likely results. These can hardly be considered to be productive in helping the ADHD child in achieving the program's goals.

One last point should be considered in implementing the program. In the example cited above, Johnny was not able to earn points for school-related behaviors on the weekend. Substituting other activities (e.g. clean his room; rake leaves; sweep the basement; etc.) so that he can make up for these lost points could be included in the system.

## The productive use of punishment

Punishment is a logical consequence following inappropriate behavior. However, like any approach, it must be administered rationally if it is to produce the desired results. It should be noted that penalties or fines on the BEHAVIOR CHART are higher than the points given for responsible behavior. This occurs for good reason. Punishment, if it is to be effective, must hurt. If this does not happen, then the ADHD child is not likely to take it seriously. Moreover, if the penalty is not severe enough, it makes it more likely that the inappropriate behavior will occur again. For example, suppose that you went out to your favorite restaurant. While trying to find a parking place, you noticed a place in front of the restaurant with a no parking sign on it. Because there were no other spaces available, you decided to take a chance and park there. At the end of the meal, you exit the restaurant and find a $2 ticket on the window. This is your punishment. Obviously, this would hardly be effective in curbing the violation the next time. In fact, the benefits that you received by violating the law far exceeded the $2 punishment, making it more likely that you would do it again. Hence, the need for appropriate intensity in administering the punishment is evident. This principle, therefore, must apply to the home point system as well. The fines should be intense enough so that the ADHD child is not likely to do this again. However, they should not be so intense that the child does not have a chance to recover.

As noted in a previous chapter, punishment is most effective when it is delivered immediately. Thus, it is recommended that no more than one warning be given if the child begins to behave badly. If the child does not respond quickly to the reprimand, the penalty must be administered forthrightly without hesitancy. In some cases, the child may have to be "timed out" or removed from the situation until he or she gains control and is ready to try again. There is little sense in punishing with several quickly administered fines for the same violation within a short period of time. This only adds fuel to the ADHD child's fire and makes matters worse. Further, it can put the child so far "into the red" that it would be virtually impossible for him or her to work his or her way out within a reasonable period of time. Therefore, the use of the "time out" is recommended. Move the child to another area until he or she calms down for about five quiet minutes. Then have him or her come back and try again. This procedure may, in some cases, have to be repeated several times and the quiet time might have to be increased. However, "time out" is usually effective in curbing the child's disruptive behavior.

### Involving the child in the program

For the most part, the home system is now in place and ready to be put into practice. However, in order for the program to work successfully, the ADHD child's cooperation is needed as well. To accomplish this objective, parents can begin by discussing their concerns with their child about his or her past performance and difficulties. They should emphasize to the child that the program is being used to help him or her so that further failure can be avoided and success can be achieved. Parents can then proceed to explain the program and how it works. The benefits of earning many rewards and how this can help the youngster to perform better at home and school should be stressed. In essence, the program needs to be presented in as positive a light as possible.

Although some children will balk because they previously received privileges non-contingently, most youngsters are able to see the benefits of the program and will cooperate. If the ADHD child is resistant, however, stick to your guns. Indicate that you are going to implement the program even though he or she is opposed to it. In fact, parents might stress that the sooner the child demonstrates competency by mastering the system, the quicker the program will be removed. This is what must be done no matter how unpleasant it might seem.

Keep in mind that oppositional children can be particularly stubborn in their refusal to comply. As noted earlier, we once had a youngster who refused to cooperate for nearly a month before he finally started to work with us. Once he began to perform successfully, his attitude changed completely. He became a strong advocate for keeping the system even when we got to the point at which we were considering eliminating it.

In the beginning stages, parents will be largely responsible for designing, implementing, and following through with the program. The child will have little, if any, input at this time. The system is being implemented because it has the potential to help the ADHD child to build needed life skills. Again, this is the point that must be emphasized with the youngster. Whether he or she likes or dislikes the program must not become the main concern. Rather, teaching the child to develop good habits and achieving future success is the primary goal.

**Behavior modification for the young child**

The preceding point system is generally effective with children between the ages of five or six and twelve to thirteen. Obviously, this would be difficult to administer with young children because it requires the ability to count and compute large numbers. However, active, impulsive children between the ages of three to five can also profit from a home behavior modification system. By setting up such a program in the early years, parents can begin by helping their child to develop good work habits and planning skills. Moreover, this will help the child to learn self-control and develop the needed confidence to function successfully at school. Thus, in working with children between the ages of three and five a more simplified behavioral system is needed. The following suggestions are offered in developing a program appropriate for this population.

First, parents should not only explain the required behaviors but they should have the child actually perform them as well. Further, when the child engages in a "big boy" or "big girl" behavior, praise should be immediately given in conjunction with some tangible reward. For example, parents can set up a game with the child called SPACE SHIP TO THE MOON. A picture of the moon and a spaceship on the Earth's surface, which is ready to embark, can be drawn on a large piece of paper. Between the Earth and the moon, a number of space stations can be inserted. Each of these takes the departing ship one step closer to the moon.

Every time the child behaves appropriately, the space ship would move forward one space. For an inappropriate behavior, the space ship would move backward one or more spaces, depending on the severity of the infraction. When the space ship arrives at the moon, a special treat such as a candy bar, chips, or some other inexpensive reward can be given.

For long-term rewards of higher value, the planets might be included on the chart with ten spaces between each planet. When the child completes the journey and arrives back to the Earth space station, a special treat may be given. Smaller treats can be provided when landing at each of the individual planets along the way. A similar approach to this might be as follows: Draw or cut out pieces of small treats (such as candy, chips, small trinkets) and special treats (such as a stuffed animal or toy) and paste these on a chart with ten spaces between each treat. A picture of the boy or girl or an actual photo of the child can be placed at the starting point. This would be moved forward or backward depending on whether the child behaved appropriately or inappropriately.

Keep in mind that the special treat (a movie) comes only after the child has engaged in responsible behavior for an extended period of time. Parents should keep in mind that any board game (for example, Candyland Bingo) provides a good format on which a child can move forward or backward, depending on his or her behavior. Remember, when the child arrives at an important point on the chart, small or big treats can be given based on how long and hard the child has worked.

Another technique, which is effective with young children, is to take a picture of a toy and cut it into a number of parts. The individual parts can then be put together like a puzzle. Each time the youngster performs successfully, one of the parts can be assembled. If the child behaves badly, one or more parts can be taken away. When the entire puzzle is completed, the youngster can go with the parents to purchase the toy.

Another very simple approach that can be used with small children is to buy a variety of stickers (cartoon or animal characters) and gold or other multi-colored stars. Take a large piece of paper and draw a picture of a "smiley face" with "Big Boy" or "Big Girl" printed on the top. Each time the child behaves responsibly, he or she can chose a sticker and paste it on the paper. A special sticker or some other favorite can be awarded when a particularly difficult task that requires extra self-control is mastered. For example, when the child works at tying his or her shoes without fussing, a special sticker might be given.

## The family meeting

Once one of the preceding programs is put into effect, it is important that it be closely monitored, particularly in the beginning stages. Therefore, a daily meeting at a specific time should be designated to discuss home and school behavior. These meetings should be mandatory and given top priority by both parents and child. Further, a maximum time limit of ten to twenty minutes should be set for each meeting depending on the age of the child. Setting a time limit helps to keep everyone on task.

During the family meetings, parents can focus on the progress that the child has made. Pointing out specific behavioral gains and the beneficial consequences can be discussed. Such meetings make it more likely that parents will consistently recognize and reinforce good habits on a daily basis. This is why the program was set up in the first place. Moreover, the family meeting will enable the parents to point out areas that need improvement. The negative consequences of inappropriate behavior might also be addressed. Finally, now that the system has been put into effect, the ADHD child's input might be sought after. Having the child comment on his progress and on the areas that need improvement can reinforce what parents are trying to accomplish. Further, by asking for the child's input, parents can determine whether the youngster truly understands the program and its purposes. Any erroneous notions can be corrected at this time.

Lastly, the family meeting provides a forum in which the child can "gripe" and share his or her frustrations about school, and/or the requirements of the program. Parents can listen to these, empathize, make recommendations, and encourage the child as needed. For the child who "hates" the program, they can reiterate that improved performance might soften their stand about the program's necessity. However, without the actual demonstration of consistently good habits over a period of time, no negotiations can occur. Caving in to the ADHD child's complaining would only put his or her future at risk for failure. Again, this may have to be pointed out very directly and firmly, particularly if he or she insists on being oppositional.

# V. DEVELOPING A BEHAVIORAL PLAN FOR THE CLASSROOM

As emphasized previously, the home and school must work together if the ADHD child's behavior and academic performance are to improve in the classroom. Daily feedback from the teacher to the parents is, in our opinion, an essential ingredient in helping the ADHD child to perform successfully in school. In fact, this is the only way in which the parents can fully support and reinforce what the classroom teacher is attempting to accomplish.

Daily feedback makes it possible to provide the needed consistency, monitoring, and accountability that leads to good learning habits. Because the classroom teacher is often overburdened, it is tempting to try to rely on weekly or bi-weekly feedback as a solution to the problem. Unfortunately, this approach is not likely to work. The feedback occurs too late or too long after the child's desirable or undesirable behavior. As a result, the administering of immediate rewards and penalties, which is essential in bringing about behavioral change, cannot be consistently applied. Again, it is daily feedback and only daily feedback that is likely to initiate the needed changes leading to improved performance. Once good habits become established, weekly and bi-weekly reports can be utilized. The child will then have acquired the necessary self-control for maintaining concentrated effort for longer periods of time without needing immediate reinforcement. However, the good habits have to be first developed before the ADHD child can be expected to sustain them.

As just indicated, providing daily feedback can be a time consuming problem for the regular classroom teacher who is responsible for monitoring many children. Thus, devising a reporting system which is simple, quick, and convenient and yet provides substantial information about the ADHD child is needed. We would propose, therefore, that a checklist, rather than a narrative report be utilized. A completed checklist that we have devised is as follows (Lavin, 1997):

## Figure 1B: Sample DAILY CLASSROOM CHECKLIST

| Name:<br>Johnny<br>Smith<br>Date:9-7-03 | Class<br>Math | Class<br>Reading | Class<br>Science | Class<br>Social<br>Studies | Class<br>Language | Class<br>Art |
|---|---|---|---|---|---|---|
| Behaviors | X | X | X | X | X | X |
| 1. Proper Materials for Class | Yes___<br>No___<br>NA___ | Yes___<br>No___<br>NA___ | Yes___<br>No___<br>NA___ | Yes___<br>No___<br>NA___ | Yes___<br>No___<br>NA___ | Yes___<br>No___<br>NA___ |
| 2. Turn in Homework | Yes___<br>No___<br>NA___ | Yes___<br>No___<br>NA___ | Yes___<br>No___<br>NA___ | Yes___<br>No___<br>NA___ | Yes___<br>No___<br>NA___ | Yes___<br>No___<br>NA___ |
| 3. Homework Neat and Accurate | Yes___<br>No___<br>NA___ | Yes___<br>No___<br>NA___ | Yes___<br>No___<br>NA___ | Yes___<br>No___<br>NA___ | Yes___<br>No___<br>NA___ | Yes___<br>No___<br>NA___ |
| 4. Follows Directions | Yes___<br>No___<br>NA___ | Yes___<br>No___<br>NA___ | Yes___<br>No___<br>NA___ | Yes___<br>No___<br>NA___ | Yes___<br>No___<br>NA___ | Yes___<br>No___<br>NA___ |
| 5. Works Properly | Yes___<br>No___<br>NA___ | Yes___<br>No___<br>NA___ | Yes___<br>No___<br>NA___ | Yes___<br>No___<br>NA___ | Yes___<br>No___<br>NA___ | Yes___<br>No___<br>NA___ |
| 6. Sits Properly | Yes___<br>No___<br>NA___ | Yes___<br>No___<br>NA___ | Yes___<br>No___<br>NA___ | Yes___<br>No___<br>NA___ | Yes___<br>No___<br>NA___ | Yes___<br>No___<br>NA___ |
| 7. Participates Properly | Yes___<br>No___<br>NA___ | Yes___<br>No___<br>NA___ | Yes___<br>No___<br>NA___ | Yes___<br>No___<br>NA___ | Yes___<br>No___<br>NA___ | Yes___<br>No___<br>NA___ |
| 8. Completes In-Class Work | Yes___<br>No___<br>NA___ | Yes___<br>No___<br>NA___ | Yes___<br>No___<br>NA___ | Yes___<br>No___<br>NA___ | Yes___<br>No___<br>NA___ | Yes___<br>No___<br>NA___ |
| 9. Enters and Leaves Properly | Yes___<br>No___<br>NA___ | Yes___<br>No___<br>NA___ | Yes___<br>No___<br>NA___ | Yes___<br>No___<br>NA___ | Yes___<br>No___<br>NA___ | Yes___<br>No___<br>NA___ |
| Homework Assignment ("none" if no work) | | | | | | |
| Teacher's Signature | | | | | | |

The reader will note that the selected behaviors, which are to be increased or decreased, are listed in numerical order on the left side of the page. At the top, in a column with separate boxes, a space for each class is provided (reading, arithmetic, language arts etc.). Under each class, blocks of Yes, No, and NA (not applicable) are placed beside the behaviors. These can be quickly checked accordingly. In a separate larger box under the "Behaviors" column, a Homework Assignment box is provided. The homework assignment for the day is inserted in this box. If there is no assigned homework, the word "none" is written. This eliminates the uncertainty as to whether the child has homework or not, which an empty box would create. Finally, a space for the teacher's signature is provided. This insures that the conveyed information is complete and accurate. It should be noted that the teacher's signature must be inserted in order for the child to obtain credit for the completed boxes for that class. If the boxes are filled in but no signature is included, the child does not get credit.

The preceding is a model checklist that can be used in the school. In applying this, the parents and teacher must decide which specific behaviors their ADHD child needs to address. These would then be inserted in numerical order under the "Behaviors" column. Next, a decision must be made on which classes need to be included in the report. These would then be listed under the "Class" heading in each row. Although there are six spaces on the sample checklist, fewer or more classes may have to be monitored, depending on the needs of the individual child.

As indicated in the previous chapter, the DAILY CLASSROOM CHECKLIST needs to be incorporated into the home based point system so that the child can be rewarded and penalized on a daily basis for his or her school performance. This can be done in the following way. The parent and teacher must decide on what constitutes a "good day" at school. Once this has been determined, then a specific number of points can be assigned for this. If the child has a "good day," then he or she receives the assigned number of points. If the day is a poor one, no points are given. For instance, on the completed sample checklist, there are six classes being monitored. For each class, there are nine designated behaviors for which the child is being held accountable. Further, the child is responsible for filling out the Homework Assignment box and obtaining the teacher's signature. In each class, therefore, there are nine Yes, No, and NA boxes, one Homework Assignment box, and Teacher Signature box to be completed. This means that eleven boxes for each of the six classes must be filled in, with a total of sixty-six boxes in all for each day.

Let's suppose that we have decided that if the child completes 80% of the possible boxes in a satisfactory manner, this would be a "good day." A satisfactory performance would mean that the Behaviors are checked Yes and the Homework Assignment and Teacher Signature boxes are filled in properly. In this case, 80% would be 53. This, therefore, means that 53 of the 66 boxes must be satisfactorily completed. A good day would earn the child ten points which would be inserted into the home chart.

We might require that an "excellent day" would require a 90% satisfactory performance. This would mean that 59 of the 66 boxes must be appropriately completed. Obviously, excellence is better than good, so the child would receive 15 points for the day.

Finally, we might then designate 25 points for a "super" or perfect day. This would require that the ADHD child complete all sixty-six items satisfactorily, thereby obtaining a 100% score. The earned points, whether they are in the "Good," "Excellent," or "Super" category, would then be incorporated into the home system and could be used to purchase rewards.

It should be noted that the preceding example is based on the possibility of all 66 boxes being completed appropriately. In other words, 54 of the 66 boxes would be checked Yes. Of the remaining 12 boxes, six would either have the correct homework assignment or "none" written in them and the last six boxes would be filled in with the teacher's signature.

It is unlikely, however, that all of the behaviors which are listed on the chart will equally apply to every class. In such cases, the NA or "not applicable" category would be checked by the teacher. For example, the art teacher may not assign homework. Thus, items number 2 and 3 would be checked NA. If NA is checked, then the number of blocks on which the daily percentage is based would be reduced. Again, let's suppose that in the art class number 2 and 3 were checked as NA. All the other boxes for each class were required to be checked as Yes or No and the Homework Assignment and Teacher Signature boxes were to be satisfactorily completed. Then the total number of blocks for which the child could receive credit would be reduced from 66 to 64. Eighty percent of 64, which now constitutes a "good day," would, therefore, be 51. "Excellent" would now be 58 and "Super" would be 64. In essence, the NA category is neutral. If it is checked, it simply lowers the number of total boxes on which the good, excellent, and super percentages are computed.

The reader will note that there are a high number of points assigned to each of these categories. This increases the likelihood that the ADHD child will be motivated to do better in school. In essence, good school performance pays well. This can be a powerful incentive to improve academic progress.

Lastly, an arrangement needs to be made to insure that the child has the checklist in his or her possession as he or she moves from class to class. Either the parents can give the checklist to the child (make sure that it is "locked" into the child's notebook so that it will not become misplaced or "lost") or arrangements can be made to have him or her pick it up from the counselor or teacher at school. It is the child's responsibility to make sure that the checklist is picked up, carried to each class, filled out properly, and returned to the parents. The child will not lose points for a poor day at school provided that a completed checklist is shown to the parents each day. However, a "forgotten," "incomplete, or "lost" checklist would result in a heavy fine, perhaps as much as 25 or 30 points per day.

It is recommended that a small number of points be given for bringing home a completed checklist, even if it is a poor one. This rewards honesty, a trait that is important in the development of a trusting parent-child relationship. Moreover, the child learns that he or she has nothing to lose by bringing home a poor sheet. It fact, it can be of benefit to him or her. The information that the sheet provides, whether it is good or bad, can be helpful. This, in fact, is its first and foremost purpose.

# VI. COORDINATION BETWEEN THE HOME AND SCHOOL

Once the home and school systems are designed, the next step is to coordinate them so that they work together. As indicated previously, the ADHD child must have the daily classroom checklist completed and returned to his or her parents in order to be rewarded accordingly. The failure to bring home the checklist would result in a heavy penalty. Because the child is rewarded for bringing home the checklist, it is always in his or her best interest to cooperate with the system. In order to demonstrate how the home and school can be coordinated, we will examine Johnny's completed weekly behavior chart and show how the information from the DAILY CLASSROOM CHECKLIST can be incorporated into the home system. The completed behavior chart is as follows:

Figure 1C: Completed Weekly BEHAVIOR CHART

See following page.

| Name Johnny Smith | | | | | | Start Date 9-7-03 | | End Date 9-14-03 | |
|---|---|---|---|---|---|---|---|---|---|
| **POSITIVE BEHAVIORS "P"** | | | | | | | | | |
| **Morning "P"** | Points | M | TU | W | TH | F | SA | SU | Weekly Total |
| 1. Ready for school 8:00 A.M. | 4 | 4 | 4 | 4 | 4 | 4 | 0 | 0 | 20 |
| 2. Eat breakfast | 4 | 4 | 4 | 4 | 4 | 4 | 4 | 4 | 28 |
| 13. Brush teeth | 3 | 3 | 3 | 3 | 3 | 3 | 3 | 3 | 21 |
| 4. Bus by 8:45 A.M. | 4 | 4 | 4 | 4 | 4 | 4 | 0 | 0 | 20 |
| **Afternoon "P"** | X | X | X | X | X | X | X | X | X |
| 1. Bring home daily school report | 5 | 5 | 0 | 5 | 5 | 5 | 0 | 0 | 20 |
| 2. Good day at school / Excellent day / Super day | 10 / 15 / 25 | 0 | 0 | 10 | 15 | 25 | 0 | 0 | 50 |
| 3. Homework done neatly and accurately | 10 | 10 | 0 | 10 | 10 | 10 | 0 | 0 | 40 |
| 4. School materials packed for next day | 5 | 5 | 5 | 5 | 5 | 5 | 0 | 0 | 25 |
| **Evening "P"** | X | X | X | X | X | X | X | X | X |
| 1. Eat supper | 4 | 4 | 4 | 4 | 4 | 4 | 4 | 4 | 28 |
| 2. Take bath | 3 | 3 | 3 | 3 | 3 | 3 | 3 | 3 | 21 |
| 3. Brush teeth | 3 | 3 | 3 | 3 | 3 | 3 | 3 | 3 | 21 |
| 4. In bed by 9:00 P.M. | 5 | 5 | 5 | 5 | 0 | 5 | 5 | 5 | 30 |
| **Daily Total "P"** | X | 50 | 40 | 30 | 60 | 85 | 52 | 59 | 324 |
| **NEGATIVE BEHAVIORS "N"** | | | | | | | | | |
| 1. Failure to bring home school report | 25 | 0 | 30 | 0 | 0 | 0 | 0 | 0 | 30 |
| 2. Failure to bring home school materials | 25 | 0 | 30 | 0 | 0 | 0 | 0 | 0 | 30 |
| 3. Disobedience | 15 | 15 | 0 | 0 | 0 | 0 | 0 | 0 | 15 |
| 4. Arguing | 10 | 10 | 10 | 0 | 10 | 0 | 0 | 0 | 30 |
| **Daily Total "N"** | X | 25 | 70 | 0 | 10 | 0 | 0 | 0 | 105 |
| **DAILY REWARDS COST "C"** | | | | | | | | | |
| 1. T.V. by the half hour | 10 | 10 | 0 | 20 | 0 | 0 | 0 | 0 | 30 |
| 2. Video game by the half hour | 10 | 10 | 0 | 10 | 0 | 10 | 0 | 0 | 30 |
| 3. Snacks | 15 | 0 | 0 | 0 | 0 | 15 | 0 | 0 | 15 |
| 4. Play game with parent | 20 | 0 | 0 | 0 | 20 | 0 | 0 | 0 | 20 |
| 5. Soda | 10 | 0 | 0 | 0 | 10 | 0 | 0 | 0 | 10 |
| 6. Ride bike by half hour | 10 | 0 | 0 | 0 | 10 | 0 | 0 | 0 | 10 |
| 7. Friend over to play | 15 | 0 | 0 | 0 | 0 | 15 | 15 | 0 | 30 |
| 8. Stay up past bedtime fifteen minutes | 15 | 0 | 0 | 0 | 0 | 15 | 0 | 15 | 30 |
| **Cost Total "C"** | X | 20 | 0 | 30 | 40 | 55 | 15 | 15 | 175 |
| **P-N-C =** | X | 5 | -30 | 0 | 10 | 30 | 37 | 44 | 44 |

required on the sample behavior chart provided earlier. However, there is a slight but substantive change in the Afternoon "P" Behaviors. Johnny is rewarded for not only bringing home the checklists, but he also receives points for "Good," "Excellent" and "Super" days at school. A good day means that Johnny completed at least 80% of the possible boxes satisfactorily; an excellent day means that 90% of the boxes were completed satisfactorily; and on a super day 100% were successfully completed.

On Monday, Johnny brought home his checklist which is as follows:

Figure 2C: Completed DAILY CLASSROOM CHECKLIST

See following page.

| Name: Johnny Smith Date:9-7-03 | Class | Class | Class | Class | Class | Class |
|---|---|---|---|---|---|---|
| | Math | Reading | Science | Social Studies | Language | Art |
| Behaviors | X | X | X | X | X | X |
| 1. Proper Materials for Class | Yes X<br>No ___<br>NA ___ | Yes X<br>No ___<br>NA ___ | Yes X<br>No ___<br>NA ___ | Yes X<br>No ___<br>NA ___ | Yes X<br>No ___<br>NA ___ | Yes X<br>No ___<br>NA ___ |
| 2. Turn in Homework | Yes X<br>No ___<br>NA ___ | Yes X<br>No ___<br>NA ___ | Yes X<br>No ___<br>NA ___ | Yes X<br>No ___<br>NA ___ | Yes X<br>No ___<br>NA ___ | Yes X<br>No ___<br>NA ___ |
| 3. Homework Neat and Accurate | Yes X<br>No ___<br>NA ___ | Yes X<br>No ___<br>NA ___ | Yes X<br>No ___<br>NA ___ | Yes ___<br>No X<br>NA ___ | Yes X<br>No ___<br>NA ___ | Yes X<br>No ___<br>NA ___ |
| 4. Follows Directions | Yes X<br>No ___<br>NA ___ | Yes X<br>No ___<br>NA ___ | Yes X<br>No ___<br>NA ___ | Yes X<br>No ___<br>NA ___ | Yes ___<br>No X<br>NA ___ | Yes X<br>No ___<br>NA ___ |
| 5. Works Properly | Yes X<br>No ___<br>NA ___ | Yes X<br>No ___<br>NA ___ | Yes X<br>No ___<br>NA ___ | Yes X<br>No ___<br>NA ___ | Yes ___<br>No X<br>NA ___ | Yes X<br>No ___<br>NA ___ |
| 6. Sits Properly | Yes ___<br>No X<br>NA ___ | Yes X<br>No ___<br>NA ___ | Yes X<br>No ___<br>NA ___ | Yes X<br>No ___<br>NA ___ | Yes X<br>No ___<br>NA ___ | Yes X<br>No ___<br>NA ___ |
| 7. Participates Properly | Yes X<br>No ___<br>NA ___ | Yes X<br>No ___<br>NA ___ | Yes X<br>No ___<br>NA ___ | Yes X<br>No ___<br>NA ___ | Yes X<br>No ___<br>NA ___ | Yes X<br>No ___<br>NA ___ |
| 8. Completes In-Class Work | Yes X<br>No ___<br>NA ___ | Yes X<br>No ___<br>NA ___ | Yes X<br>No ___<br>NA ___ | Yes X<br>No ___<br>NA ___ | Yes X<br>No ___<br>NA ___ | Yes X<br>No ___<br>NA ___ |
| 9. Enters and Leaves Properly | Yes ___<br>No X<br>NA ___ | Yes X<br>No ___<br>NA ___ | Yes X<br>No ___<br>NA ___ | Yes X<br>No ___<br>NA ___ | Yes X<br>No ___<br>NA ___ | Yes ___<br>No X<br>NA ___ |
| Homework Assignment ("none" if no work) | Book Pages 14-15 | None | None | Work-sheet Capitals | None | Study pages 17-18 (book) |
| Teacher's Signature | *Ms. Hughes* | *Mr. Johnson* | | *Ms. Simpson* | *Ms. Walker* | *Mr. Rhodes* |

66 boxes satisfactorily, earning a total score of 72%. While Johnny was rewarded for bringing home the daily checklist, he received no points for a "good day" at school. It should be noted that Johnny lost credit for ten successfully completed blocks because the teacher's signature was missing for the science class. Again, without teacher verification, no credit could be given. In fact, Johnny's arguing and disobedience, which occurred with his parents following this, cost him an additional 25 points.

On Tuesday, Johnny decided to test the limits. He "lost" the checklist and, as the BEHAVIOR CHART shows, he received no points for bringing it home to his parents. Because he provided no school information for that day, he also lost "good day" at school and homework points as well. Moreover, Johnny was penalized 30 points for not bringing home the checklist and not having information about homework assignments for the next day. Thus, a sixty-point penalty on top of losing forty possible additional school-related behavior points occurred. Obviously, this combined loss was substantial and painful.

On Wednesday, Johnny complied with the system. As the BEHAVIOR CHART indicates, he not only remembered to bring home the checklist but he had a "good day" at school as well, completing 54 of the 66 blocks successfully (82%). This earned him 10 additional points, which were incorporated into the behavior chart at home. In fact, Johnny would have had a perfect day. Because he failed to bring home his Tuesday checklist, however, he did not know the homework assignments that were due on Wednesday. As a result, on Wednesday's checklist he lost all credit for items 2 and 3 on the behaviors section of the DAILY CLASSOOM CHECKLIST.

On Thursday and Friday, Johnny continued to make significant school improvement. Thursday's checklist showed that he had an "excellent day," successfully completing 92% of the blocks (59 of 64). It should be noted that on Wednesday, no homework was assigned in language class, therefore items 2 and 3 were checked NA. Thus, the percentage was computed on 64 instead of 66 completed blocks. Johnny's 92% earned him an additional 15 points on the home BEHAVIOR CHART.

As the BEHAVIOR CHART shows, Johnny had a perfect day on Friday. He completed all 66 of the blocks successfully, earning 25 points for a 100% score.

By the middle of the week, Johnny had clearly grasped how the system worked. His cooperation resulted not only in the earning of extra points but an over-all better school performance occurred as well. In fact, despite spending for daily rewards as the behavior chart shows, Johnny had 44 points left over. These were used to purchase a CERTIFICATE OF DEPOSIT from the bank on 9-14-03. The amount of 44 points was credited toward having a friend spend the night at Johnny's house. The cost for this reward was 250 points, leaving a balance of 206 points to be paid.

As the preceding charts suggest, Johnny now has the potential to obtain both daily and long-term rewards. Moreover, the close monitoring of teachers and parents has enabled him to perform better at home and school.

# VII. RESPONSE-COST: AN APPROACH FOR "HASSLED" PARENTS

## Overview

Response cost can be a very effective tool for modifying the ADHD child's behavior (Goldstein & Goldstein, 1990; Kaufman & O'Leary, 1972; Lavin, 2003; Mickenbaum, 1977; Rapport, Murphy, & Bailey, 1982; Rapport, 1987). Response cost works like this. The ADHD child is first provided with the full range of all possible privileges at the onset of the program. The child is told that he or she will be allowed to keep these privileges provided that he or she behaves appropriately. Specific inappropriate behaviors are then specified (lying, stealing, cussing etc.). It is explained to the youngster that if he or she engages in any of these acts of wrongdoing, one, two, or more of these privileges will be taken away for a period of time.

For example, Johnny is allowed to stay up until 9:30 p.m. if he behaved appropriately for that day. However, each time that he disobeys, talks back, or fails to do what he is told, 10 minutes is to be taken off his bedtime. On Monday, Johnny cusses twice and disobeys once. Three infractions have occurred. Therefore, Johnny is sent to bed at 9 p.m. He then starts over with a clean slate on Tuesday.

Another example might help here. Sally is given an allowance of $4 per week. The $4, in quarters, is put into a jar and placed on the top of the refrigerator. If Sally commits no violations between Monday and Sunday, she receives the entire amount of money. However, should Sally engage in any inappropriate behavior, twenty-five cents is to be taken away for each infraction.

It should be noted that response cost can work particularly well with ADHD children who have a long history of failure. Some have been put on behavior modification programs using rewards in an attempt to motivate them. However, many ADHD youngsters have great difficulty controlling themselves long enough to earn these rewards. They, therefore, develop a pessimistic attitude, believing that it is unlikely that they will ever be successful no matter how hard they try. Hence, a program requiring good behavior before earning rewards is not motivating to them.

Because they have been so unsuccessful in attempting to earn rewards, many ADHD youngsters perform much better when privileges are given to them in advance. It is more likely that they will behave appropriately to keep what they have, rather than to try to earn something that they don't believe it is possible to attain. Moreover, by using the response-cost approach, the program can be structured so that all privileges are not taken away when a violation occurs. Rather, some privileges are still available, provided that the youngster recoups and refrains from further infractions. Such an approach leaves the child with some "hope," making it more likely that he or she will not quit trying.

For parents, the benefits of using response cost are many. First, it often requires less record keeping than that which is needed to implement a daily positive reinforcement behavior modification program. Second, because inappropriate behavior is usually quite disruptive, parents are more likely to attend to it. This, in turn, increases the likelihood that immediate and consistent consequences will be applied and that more appropriate behavior will follow. Third, response cost requires that the consequences for violations be determined before these occur. This makes it more likely that "the punishment will fit the crime," so to speak. As a result, disciplinary overreactions, complaints about unfairness, power struggles, and family dissention can be minimized and even avoided. Moreover, as mentioned earlier, for the ADHD child who has a chronic history of failure, a response-cost program can provide an ongoing incentive for continuing to cooperate with his or her parents. The increase in appropriate behavior resulting from this can serve as an antidote to discouragement. The ADHD child's behavioral improvement will certainly be noticed by other people. This, therefore, can bring praise from peers, parents, and teachers, making it even more likely that the youngster will want to do well in the future.

**Constructing the response-cost program**

As indicated previously, the first task is to present to the child the full range of rewards and privileges that will be made available to him or her. These are divided into three categories: DAILY, WEEKLY, and LONG-TERM. Daily rewards are those that would be available to the child each day during the seven-day week. Examples of these as follows:

### *DAILY REWARDS/PRIVILEGES*

Television
Stereo
Video Games
Telephone
Snacks
Stay Up Until _____
Play Game with Parent
Parent Read a Story
Ride Bike
Soft Drink
Go for Walk/Ride with Parent
Ice Cream
Friend to Play
Draw, Paint, Make Crafts
Help Mom with Dinner

The child and the parents can add to the preceding list. Again, these daily rewards and privileges are those which can be made available seven days a week, provided that no violations occur. The use of the daily rewards and privileges is determined within restrictions imposed by the parents. For instance, the child might be limited to one soft drink per day and to one hour of playing video games each day. Parents should use good judgment in this regard.

## WEEKLY REWARDS/PRIVILEGES

Fast Food Restaurant
Go to Library
Special Dessert
Visit Friend for Day
Out for Ice Cream
Allowance for Week
Friend Overnight
Special Meal at Home
Pizza
Rollerblading
Ice Skating
Movie
Visit Grandparent for Day or Weekend

Again, the child and parents can add to this list. If the child commits no violations for the week, the preceding privileges, provided that they do not conflict with other obligations and can be made available during the weekend, may be chosen by the child. Keep in mind that making sure that some of these are available for a week of no violations rewards good behavior. This, of course, is what you want to increase.

## LONG-TERM (TWO WEEKS OR MORE) REWARDS/PRIVILEGES

Expensive Restaurant
Buy a Video Game
Buy a Ten Dollar Toy
Fishing
Professional Sporting Event
Amusement Park
Picnic at Park
Buy Clothes
Take a Friend to a Movie, Ballgame or Restaurant
Go to Arcade
Day Trip to Place of Child's Choice
Go to Zoo

For two weeks or more of no violations, these "super" rewards can be made available, provided that parents have the means and time to do so. Weekly and long-term privileges can be discussed in advance with the child. Again, no violations for a specific period of time are what make these available.

Once the rewards and privileges have been determined, then all inappropriate behaviors which could result in losing these would be identified and put into three categories: EXTREMELY SERIOUS, VERY SERIOUS, and SERIOUS. It should be explained to the child that if he or she engages in any of these behaviors, one, two, or more of these privileges can be taken away, depending on the seriousness of the offense.

EXTREMELY SERIOUS violations are those in which the rights of others are violated, resulting in damage to or the loss of property, injury to other persons, or a major inconvenience to those who are responsible for caring for the child. Extremely serious violations require that the child does the following: (1) apologize for the violation; (2) make restitution for the loss, damage, or injury; and (3) pay a "fine" or perform community service. If an extremely serious violation occurs, then all privileges for the day, week, and long term are suspended until the preceding is completed. Once this occurs, privileges would resume as usual. Examples of extremely serious violations and what must be done to rectify them are as follows:

1. Stealing from a store, parent, teacher or member of the community
   a) Return or pay for the item.
   b )Apologize for the "antisocial" act.
   c) Perform a service for the inconvenience or disruption that was caused by this.

2. Destroying property
   a) Apologize to the property owner.
   b )Fix or pay for the damage.
   c) Perform a service for the institution or person whose property was destroyed.

3.   Hitting and/or injuring another person
     a) Apologize.
     b) Pay for any medical treatment.
     c) Perform a service for the person.

4.   Cheating and lying
     a) Apologize to the affected person.
     b) Go to each person whose life has been inconvenienced by the lie or act of cheating and tell the truth.
     c) Pay back or perform a service for those whose lives have been negatively affected.

5.   School suspension
     a) Apologize verbally and in writing for the violation.
     b) Make restitution to those affected.
     c) Provide a service for those whose lives have been inconvenienced.

In order that the child might understand the rationale for the preceding, the following explanation, from your perspective as a parent, can be given: "If I stole something from a store and I was caught, I would be required to apologize for my mistake, pay back or return the item, and go to court because I broke the law. The judge would make me pay a fine, perform community service, or he might send me to jail. When you break an important rule, the same consequences apply to you. This is only fair. This is why we are requiring you to do this. Once you complete your obligations, then all of your privileges will be restored." Such an explanation helps the child to understand that the consequences are sensible and not arbitrarily applied. Moreover, it provides the ADHD child with specifics as to what is required and when his or her privileges will be returned. This is the kind of structure to which ADHD children are most likely to respond.

VERY SERIOUS VIOLATIONS are those in which the rights of others have been violated but there is no loss or damage of property, injury to others, or major disruptions that occur. Very serious violations frequently occur during the child's interaction with persons of authority such as parents and teachers. The following would be considered to be very serious violations:

1.  Disobedience
2.  Refusal to comply with a parent or teacher's request the first time
3.  Arguing
4.  Cursing
5.  Back talk
6.  Refusal to follow the parent or teacher's rules and standards of behavior (e.g., ready for school by 8 a.m.; eat properly at the table; proper grooming and dress).

Children have a moral obligation to respect the authority of parents and teachers. They owe them obedience, courtesy, and compliance to reasonable requests. Failure to respond accordingly, therefore, is a very serious infraction which requires that corrective consequences be immediately applied.

Should a very serious violation occur, then a portion of one or more of the child's daily privileges are removed. If the child stops the inappropriate behavior, he or she will still have a right to the remaining portion of a privilege or the other privileges that are still available for that day. Should the behavior continue, a suitable warning might be given before enacting another penalty. The parent, for example, might say: "Please stop this behavior now. Otherwise I will have to take ten more minutes off your bed time." If the child persists despite the warning and the removal of another privilege, then all privileges are suspended for that day. The child's blatant failure to comply now becomes an extremely serious violation, requiring an apology and the expressed willingness to try to do better the next day. For example, the child should be required to state: "I'm sorry for my behavior. I will try to do better tomorrow." Once the child sincerely apologizes and commits him or herself to making a better effort, then all privileges are restored on the following day. Again, this serves as an antidote to discouragement and makes it more likely that the child will be cooperative with his or her parents.

SERIOUS VIOLATIONS are those in which the child, rather than other persons, is inconvenienced or injured as a result of his or her inappropriate behavior. The child is required to correct the mistake so that his or her life can get "back on track" and he or she can function normally once more. As indicated earlier, a persistent failure to correct this behavior could become a very serious or an extremely serious violation, depending on the inconvenience or damage to others that might ensue. Some examples of serious violations and the consequences that might be applied are as follows:

1. Losing or forgetting homework
   a) The child must make up the work. Then, all privileges are restored.
2. Pouting or refusing to talk when asked a question or spoken to
   a) Ignore the child until he or she decided to respond.
   b) All privileges are restored when the child quits pouting.
3. Fails to clean room or pick up toys
   a) All privileges are taken away until the task is completed.
   b) The child could choose to have the parent pick up the toys. However, the toys would then become the parent's property. The parents will keep the toys or dispose of them as they see fit.
4. Picking at food, eating too slowly or exhibiting poor table manners
   a) Set short time limit (e.g. one minute) to correct the behavior.
   b) If not corrected, confiscate the food.
   c) No dessert or snack
   d) The child will receive no food until the next scheduled meal. If this occurs in the evening, this means no food until the next morning.
5. Failing to dress or groom him or herself properly (e.g. brush teeth, comb hair, bathe, etc.)
   a) The child will be sent to bed earlier. This will ensure that he or she is up in time to attend to these tasks the next morning.

**Behavioral principles for response-cost**

In a previous discussion of behavioral principles, the fact that a child will not engage in inappropriate behavior so that he or she can avoid potentially negative consequences was briefly focused upon. For example, the child might sit quietly in order to avoid losing the privilege of watching TV with the family. Or in order to avoid receiving a failing grade, he or she might complete missing homework assignments and give these to the teacher just before the term ends. In both cases, these youngsters actually behaved appropriately because they wanted to avoid negative consequences. When there is an increase in some desirable behavior in order to avoid such consequences, then negative reinforcement occurs. Like positive reinforcement (in which desirable behavior is followed by pleasant consequences), negative reinforcement also increases the frequency of behavior. In the first example, the child maintains good self-control so that the pleasure of watching TV with the family is not taken away. In the second example, an increase in study behavior occurs so that a failing grade for the term can be avoided.

Another factor that needs to be taken into account in using response cost is the application of punishment. For example, if a tantruming child is removed from class and placed in a time-out room and the tantrum ceases, then the time-out is truly an effective punishment. However, if the tantrum continues, the time-out is not a punishment because the child's negative behavior did not stop. So if a punishment is really effective, it will cause the ADHD child to terminate what he or she is doing.

Moreover, the child will now, more than likely, behave appropriately in order to avoid being punished in the future. When the child increases desirable behavior so that a punishment can be avoided, then negative reinforcement has occurred. It is this combination of using punishment and negative reinforcement upon which response cost is based. Again, even though the reinforcers are negative, like positive reinforcers, the proper use of these will help to improve the ADHD child's work habits and overall behavior.

## Making the school a part of the response-cost program

Daily feedback from the ADHD child's classroom teacher can be woven into the home response-cost program. The child can be required to bring home the daily checklist that was described in the previous chapter. Since the ADHD child's performance in school is a serious matter, bringing the checklist home and making sure that it is filled out properly are of the utmost importance. Also, making sure that the child has fulfilled his or her educational obligations and met appropriate behavioral standards are important. Should the youngster fail to meet these requirements, then corrective action must be taken.

Because the child's "job" is to become an educated and productive citizen, the failure to bring home the checklist should be considered a VERY SERIOUS VIOLATION. While the child is only injuring him or herself by this behavior, it is an act of disobedience and a failure to comply with a parental request. Moreover, not bringing home the checklist could be an act of lying. The child might claim that he "forgot" or "lost" the checklist. However, the truth might be that he was just attempting to avoid accepting responsibility for a bad day. Such deception cannot be tolerated. If this occurs, therefore, all privileges for the day are to be suspended. The repeated failure to respond to this request could eventually become an EXTREMELY SERIOUS VIOLATION. If the child refuses to comply for a week, let's say, then all privileges are to be curtailed until an apology is made, all work is made up, and a service is performed for inconveniencing the parents and teachers who have to engage in extra work as a result of the child's negligence.

If the checklist is brought home each day and the child has failed to complete assignments, then these must be made up. As soon as they are completed and satisfactorily turned in, all privileges are restored.

With regard to behavioral standards, as indicated in the previous chapter, a minimum standard of 80% of the possible acceptable checks constitutes a good day. Should the child fall below the 80% minimum, then one or more of the privileges for the day might be removed. For example, if the youngster's overall score fell within the 70% range, a portion or a minor privilege might be taken away. However, if only a 25% score occurred, then all privileges for the day might be lost. For scores above 80%, in the 90% to 100% range, an extra privilege could be made available. Generally, however, at least an 80% minimum would be required with no violations for that day. Keep in mind that a string of consecutive no violation days is needed in order to obtain weekly and long-term rewards and privileges.

In evaluating the child's performance from the classroom checklist, good judgment in determining how much should be taken away when standards are not met needs to be exercised. A point between being too harsh and too lenient needs to be determined in implementing this aspect of the program. Otherwise, the ADHD child can become quickly discouraged and quit trying to behave appropriately at home because of problems occurring at school. If this occurs, a conference with the child's teachers and a behavioral plan to correct this needs to be put into practice.

In summation, the response-cost approach provides the ADHD child with a full range of privileges which can only be lost if he or she behaves inappropriately. In other words, the child does not have to first earn these. Rather, they are given freely, provided that no violations occur. Should an infraction result, the rewards and privileges are taken away. Once the appropriate corrections are made, these are once more restored in their entirety.

The response-cost approach, as noted earlier, provides an ongoing incentive for the ADHD child to cooperate with his or her parents. This ultimately leads to not only better behavior, but it increases the likelihood that the ADHD youngster will receive positive feedback from parents, teachers, and peers. This, in turn, makes it more likely that good work habits and socially appropriate behavior will continue.

# VIII. COPING WITH RESISTANCE UNDERMINING YOUR BEHAVIOR MODIFICATION SYSTEM

Even well designed behavior modification programs run into snags which can render them ineffective. Usually human factors, not the system itself, cause this to happen. More specifically, resistance from the child, the teachers, and the parents themselves can undermine the potential effectiveness of even the best-conceived programs. If these resistances are not overcome, then the system will not work. Oftentimes, behavior modification gets blamed for the failure rather than those who are responsible for implementing it. We have frequently heard parents say, "I've tried that (behavior modification) and it doesn't work." In inquiring further, we have often discovered that it wasn't behavior modification that was responsible for the failure. Rather, the reasons for the program's demise were that teachers were unwilling to provide daily feedback; the system wasn't "tight" enough so that the child was held accountable throughout the day; the parents weren't consistent in administering the program; the child would intentionally behave badly, trying to discourage the parents into dissolving the program; or the child would engage the parents in a "power struggle" in order to get even with them for some perceived injustice from the past (this might occur when children are caught in loyalty conflicts or the bickering between parents who are separated or divorced).

The latter can be particularly problematic because some children are so hurt and angry that they are willing to ruin their lives by behaving poorly. The purpose of this disintegration is to intentionally aggravate their parents and to force their parents to attend to them. In fact, this tactic is often successful. Because parents do get extremely upset and pay an undue amount of attention to this disintegration, inadvertently such behavior is actually being rewarded. Therefore, the program is likely to be rejected, and the system never gets the chance to get off the ground so to speak. Such a power struggle must be diffused if the program is to work successfully. In order to focus on these resistances and the special problems associated with each, a discussion of the "roadblocks" erected by the child, the teacher, and the parents will be treated separately. This will enable the reader to examine the causes of the problem and overcoming these resistances in greater depth.

## The child

As indicated earlier, the child might be resistant to the program because, prior to its inception, he or she may have received privileges without any contingencies attached to them. It is not unusual for such a youngster to "kick up his heels" when he is now being required to behave appropriately in order to receive rewards that were once freely given. Depending on the stubbornness of the child, such rebellion, which is manifested by a refusal to comply with the system, could last for some time. However, it is important not to get faint-hearted when this occurs. Parents must not cave in to this intimidation. In fact, if they give in, they will be rewarding the very behavior that they are trying to curb. It is important to stick with the system for three or four weeks, even if the child throughout this time refuses to comply. Continue to conduct family meetings, remain consistent, and above all encourage the child by letting him know that you care about him. You may want to make some minor corrections (lower the point cost for some of the rewards) to suit the child, but again, don't modify the basic structure, principles, or accountability. Most ADHD children will see the wisdom of what you are doing and they will eventually comply, realizing that it is in their best interest to do so. If the oppositional behavior continues beyond three or four weeks, professional help might be sought.

One other point must be kept in mind. As noted earlier, some ADHD children will refuse to comply with the system because they want to hurt or to take out their anger on one or both parents. Their disintegration is designed to purposely upset the parents in order to obtain attention and to gain control over them in negative ways. This frequently leads to "power struggles" and senseless, illogical arguing and fighting. If this is occurring, then those emotional factors that are sabotaging the system must be identified and diffused so that the program can function successfully. Again, this might require professional help so that all parties can clear the air and overcome the negative feelings that are preventing the system from working.

**The teacher**

No home-school system can be successful without the cooperation of the classroom teacher. The teacher's daily feedback is essential to making the program work effectively. It is important to keep in mind that the regular classroom teacher is responsible for supervising as many as twenty-five to thirty or more children. This can be very time-consuming, demanding, and emotionally stressful. Just having one ADHD child in the group can significantly add to this already difficult responsibility.

Parents should try to understand the teacher's point of view and avoid being accusatory or demanding in their attempt to obtain his or her cooperation. The overriding majority of teachers enter the profession hoping to make a difference in the lives of their students. They want children to learn and they want to believe that their efforts have contributed to the child's progress. The educational improvement of their youngsters is, in essence, the teacher's reward.

When seeking the cooperation of the classroom teachers, it is important to let them know that their efforts are absolutely necessary to the improvement of the ADHD child's performance. Parents must clearly communicate that they understand that teachers have numerous responsibilities and that filling out a daily classroom checklist is an added burden. However, it should be stressed that this is the only way that the ADHD child can be consistently held accountable, and it is the only way that parents can fully support the teachers in achieving their goals for the child. Weekly, biweekly, or monthly feedback is unlikely to be effective. Such feedback comes too late. By the time it is received, it is unlikely that the child will be able to catch up on missed work and then move forward. Parents might even agree to send the checklist back to the school with their signature to acknowledge that they received it and that the results have been recorded on the behavior chart. In this way, the teachers will know that their contributions are making a difference. Moreover, it lets the teachers know that parents appreciate their extra effort and cooperation.

If, despite the parents' best efforts, a teacher refuses to cooperate, there is little sense in becoming accusatory or vindictive. This would not be in the child's best interest. Rather, it would be best to consult with a higher authority about having the child placed in another class with a teacher who is willing to help. If this cannot be accomplished, then making the best of the situation might be the only alternative available. Parents may have to settle for weekly, biweekly, or monthly feedback and incorporate this into the system accordingly. If parents have the resources, they may want to consider placing their child in a private school that would accommodate them. Again, professional advice regarding this matter might be sought.

## The parents

Parents must keep in mind that behavior modification is founded on principles that have a proven track record of working successfully when properly applied. If the program is not working, identifying the "bugs" in the system and eliminating these is of particular importance. These "bugs" might be a lack of parental consistency, parental disagreements about methods or goals which are aired in the child's presence, making the attainment of rewards too easy or too difficult, parental discouragement and giving up too quickly when adversity arises, or the child's intentional sabotaging of the system which was discussed previously.

Whatever the reason for the failure, blaming the system will not alter or improve the ADHD child's behavior. Placing blame on behavior modification may make parents temporarily feel better. It can serve as an excuse to avoid dealing with the rigorous challenges of getting to the root of the problem and making needed changes. Moreover, a failed system can inadvertently be used by some parents to vindicate themselves because they feel guilty. They can conclude that they "have tried everything" and "nothing works." They might further conclude that their ADHD child is doomed by his or her biological make-up and that there isn't anything that can be done to compensate for this. Unfortunately, such a negative outlook leads to despair or the overreliance on medication to cope with the ADHD child's difficulties. Parents must be on guard against falling into such cynicism. If they trouble-shoot appropriately, make a diligent effort and remain optimistic, the program is likely to be successful.

# IX. COGNITIVE RESTRUCTURING: THE IMPORTANCE OF TEACHING THE ADHD CHILD TO THINK CONSTRUCTIVELY

## Why cognitive restructuring is so important

ADHD children usually have low self-esteem, an inability to cope with frustration, and poor self-control. ADHD children often do not stop to think. Rather, they behave impulsively, failing to control their actions. Because such behavior naturally draws negative attention to them, they frequently develop feelings of incompetence (Cotugno, 1995; Erik, 1995,1997; Gresham & Elliott, 1984; McConnel & Odom, 1986). Moreover, their impulsivity interferes with their capacity to learn in school and to establish viable relationships with peers and persons in authority (Erk,2000).

ADHD children can be quite oppositional and act out accordingly. This occurs because they become frustrated with themselves, believing that they are incapable of controlling their behavior and the events impacting on their lives (Bandura,1977; Weiner, 1979). It is not surprising, therefore, that they develop an "external locus of control," thinking that luck, outside events, or other people are largely responsible for what happens to them (Dweck, 1975; Licht et. al., 1985; Linn & Hodge, 1982; Rosenbaum & Baker, 1984). ADHD children who take medication can be particularly prone to such kind of thinking. As noted earlier, they oftentimes attribute their success or failure to whether they did or did not take their pills that day (Lavin, 1989; Walen & Henker, 1976). Obviously, children who think in this vein are unlikely to take responsibility for their actions, believing that they are incompetent and inferior to others. As a result, they tend to continue to engage in dysfunctional behavior. This, in turn, leads to more failure and negative feedback from peers and those adults who teach and care for them.

In order for the child to acquire self-confidence, a change in his or her views about self, life, and other people must occur. An "internal," rather than an "external locus of control," must be fostered. In other words, the youngster needs to take responsibility for his or her actions, believing that he or she, not luck, outside events, or other people, are responsible for the consequences that follow. Such a change in thinking can be accomplished, if positive rather than negative self-attributions are emphasized (Dweck, 1975; Reid & Borkowski, 1987). Positive, productive thoughts can serve as a mediator, modifying the child's negative affect (anxiety, depression, frustration) and those impulsive overreactions that often follow (Heinker, Walen, & Henshaw, 1980).

For example, when Louis is required to complete a math assignment, he repeatedly says to himself, "There is no sense trying. I'll fail anyway. Math is impossible. It's just too difficult for a stupid person like me." Obviously, these thoughts would cause Louis to become despondent and to engage in considerable self-pity, leading to increasing frustration. This might then be followed by withdrawal, whining, defensiveness, and oppositional behavior. If Louis continued to think in this vein, it is unlikely that he would ever perform competently in math or in any other academic area that was challenging for him.

However, let's suppose that Louis learned to view himself differently, in a more positive and realistic light. Suppose he started to make statements to himself such as, "Math is difficult for me but I can complete it satisfactorily if I make the effort. I'm certainly not stupid. If I try, I will like myself a lot better than if I become a quitter." This kind of thinking makes it more likely that Louis would feel more hopeful and even optimistic. This, in turn, would lead to better attending behavior and a more concentrated work effort. Louis would now be on the way to developing an "internal locus of control."

More productive thinking can help the ADHD child to view him or herself as someone who can achieve successfully rather than a powerless victim who is incapable of self-control. While learning this skill is not an easy task, with motivation, practice, and repetition, it will eventually become a "cognitive habit," so to speak. Productive thinking can be of the utmost importance in improving the ADHD child's self-confidence and the willingness to assume responsibility for making good choices. Hence, the development of an "internal locus of control," which is an essential ingredient to good self-esteem, can eventually become an integral part of the ADHD child's personality.

## Cognitive restructuring with the ADHD child

It should be kept in mind that ADHD children often have a different mind set than that of their ordinary peer group. Many of them have been told that their ADHD is genetically or biochemically based. While there is certainly a body of evidence to support this (Erk, 2000), it can cause ADHD children to believe that there is little or nothing that they can do to control their behavior. As noted earlier, for those children who take medication, success or failure can be attributed to ingesting or not ingesting "the pill." The ADHD child might insist that without the pill to correct his or her "chemical imbalance," self-control is virtually impossible. It is this mind set which must be challenged. Otherwise, this can become the excuse for failure. The child needs to learn that despite ADHD, he or she can take positive steps in controlling attention and impulsivity. Medication can be helpful but it is only an adjunct, not the cause of good performance. Rather, the child must learn to believe that his or her efforts, regardless of any biochemical underpinnings, determine whether success or failure occurs.

## The first step in cognitive restructuring: Building trust

In order for cognitive restructuring to occur, the ADHD child must be receptive to making changes in his or her thinking. As noted earlier, ADHD children become quite oppositional and defensive when criticized by others. Because their feelings are easily hurt (which they are unlikely to admit), they are quick to overreact. They are, therefore, often unlikely to listen to what even the most sincere caregivers have to say. Rather, excuse making, blaming, and arguing take place, despite the fact one might be genuinely trying to help them. If the ADHD child is going to be receptive to what is taught, he or she must view the caregiver in a positive light. In other words, the child must perceive the caregiver as an ally, not an "enemy" who must be defended against at all cost. Such a change in view makes it more likely that the youngster will be open to the caregiver's suggestions and restructure his or her thoughts accordingly.

Building a trusting relationship with the ADHD child is, therefore, the first step in implementing cognitive restructuring. Again, the caregiver must remember that ADHD children have often been chastised and criticized with much frequency. As a result, they are quick to conclude that others are "against" them. If this perception is to be changed, it is of the utmost importance that the caregiver demonstrates that he or she is able to empathize with the ADHD child's plight (Erk, 2000; Lambert & Cattani-Thompson, 1996). Clearly communicating to the child that ADHD was acquired by factors beyond his or her control, not a condition brought on by a conscious choice, can help. Moreover, letting the child know that being diagnosed with ADHD would be frustrating for anyone would be beneficial. After all, the majority of youngsters are not cursed with this affliction. As a result, they appear to have a much easier time learning in school and getting along with peers, teachers, and other adults.

By empathizing with the ADHD child, two purposes can be achieved. First, empathy enables the caregiver to build rapport with the youngster. Second, this makes it more likely that the child will be receptive to and integrate that which is communicated to him or her. In order to demonstrate empathy, the caregiver might state something like the following:

"You are right about ADHD being a problem that causes difficulty for you. It is frustrating because you didn't choose to have ADHD. It seems that people are always acting like it's your fault because you have trouble with self-control. The real reason why you have trouble controlling yourself is that you have more energy than most people. This is something that you were born with, not something you intentionally caused to happen. So when you fidget, become distracted, or react quickly without thinking, it is because this uncontrollable energy is influencing you to behave in this way. Most people don't understand this. And when they criticize you, it hurts and is irritating because you believe that it is unfair to be blamed for something that you can't help."

By communicating empathy in this manner, the ADHD child is more likely to perceive the caregiver as a trustworthy advocate, someone who does not only understand but also may be able to help him or her with self-control problems. In order to achieve the latter, the following might be added to the preceding. This will enable the youngster to see that he or she can learn to gain control and to manage their seemingly boundless energy.

"As I just indicated, you have more energy than most people. Actually, having lots of energy is a good thing. If you use this energy properly, you could achieve much more than those people who are less energetic than yourself. You might think of your body as an automobile and your brain as the motor which runs and drives it. Your body contains this large reservoir of gasoline or energy which powers your automobile. The trick for you is to learn how to wisely use your 'high test' gasoline so that your automobile runs smoothly and efficiently.

"As you know, every automobile has an accelerator. When we push down on the peddle, it regulates the amount of gas that enters the motor. This is what makes it go faster or slower. If we push the peddle too hard, too much gasoline causes the automobile to go out of control. If we fail to push the peddle hard enough, then the automobile won't move or it will go too slowly.

"Going back to what I said earlier, the trick for you is to learn to regulate your 'high-powered' energy so that you can be successful at home and school. You might think of your brain as being the accelerator that runs your body. If you control your brain, or what you think, then you could make sure that your automobile goes at the right speed, not too fast and not too slow. What do you think about what I am saying?"

At this point, the caregiver can then affirm whether the child's perception about what has been conveyed is correct or whether further explanation is needed. Once the preceding is completed, the caregiver can move forward in instructing the ADHD child on how to apply cognitive restructuring so that he or she can gain better self-control.

"Keep in mind that your brain is the accelerator that controls your behavior. If you think good thoughts, then you will feel happier and make better choices. If you think bad thoughts, then you will be frustrated and behave foolishly and get yourself into trouble. For example, suppose that you believe this: 'I have ADHD. Therefore, I am a stupid person.' How do you think that you are going to feel? (Pause and let the child respond or continue.) That's right! You would feel dumb and inadequate in comparison to your classmates. And if you believe that you are dumb, how will you behave? (Pause and let the child respond.) That's correct.

You're not going to try to do the work and you'll be uncooperative when the teacher tries to make you complete it. In fact, some children even argue with the teacher or act up in goofy ways so that they can avoid doing the assignments. What do you think about that?" Once more, the caregiver concludes with a question in order to obtain the child's input so that any errors in perception can be corrected.

**The second step: Cognitive restructuring**

Following this introduction, the caregiver is then ready to begin working with the ADHD child keeping two objectives in mind. First, those misperceptions which are particularly common to ADHD children need to be specifically identified. Second, specific productive thoughts must then be generated. Those counter productive thoughts (CP), which we have found to be particularly prevalent with ADHD youngsters, and their productive (P) replacements are as follows:

(CP1) I have ADHD. This means that I am dumb and stupid in comparison to my classmates.

(P1) Because you have ADHD doesn't mean that you are dumb and stupid. In fact, ADHD children are just as smart as their classmates. Having ADHD means that you have more energy than most people. You have trouble controlling this energy. That's the problem. You have plenty of "brain power." However, your only problem is learning to make use of this properly.

(CP2) Having ADHD is unfair. It is not my fault that I have this problem. I didn't choose to be this way. Peers and adults should understand this and stop criticizing and blaming me.

(P2) You are right that you didn't choose to have ADHD. Of course, you believe that having ADHD is unfair and that people should "get off your case" about it. Unfortunately, life itself is unfair. Almost everyone has a problem. (Give an example.) For example, Louis has trouble throwing and catching a ball. The boys make fun of him because of this. However, he can't help it. You think that having lots of energy is unfair. However, if you learn to control this energy and use it wisely, then you could actually do better than other people. This is something you could fix if you are willing to make the effort.

(CP3) I have a "chemical imbalance." Because of this, I am incapable of controlling myself. This is why I take pills. Without pills, there is nothing I can do to control my behavior.

(P3) Pills can help to calm you by slowing your motor down. However, it is using your brain and learning to think correctly that is most important in helping you to gain control of yourself. When you learn to control yourself, then you will feel proud because you have made the right choice and behaved appropriately. You are responsible for this, not "the pill."

(CP4) When something is difficult for me, I shouldn't have to do it. After all, I have ADHD and I can't help getting frustrated when hard tasks are assigned to me.

(P4) While it is true that having ADHD is frustrating, it doesn't mean that you can't overcome the frustration and complete the task. The chances are that your teachers and parents give you tasks that you are actually capable of completing, if you calm yourself and make the effort. In fact, by overcoming your frustration and completing the assignment, you will be demonstrating good self-control. This will make you proud because you will be doing this using your own brain power in controlling your energy.

(CP5) Because I have ADHD other kids tease and make fun of me. They call me "hyper" and other bad names. People in authority should stop the teasing and severely punish them for hurting my feelings. They should always protect me.

(P5) You are right that other kids say mean things. Some may even try to hurt your feelings by making fun of you. Teachers can punish them when they are caught teasing you. However, this won't solve the problem. Rather, how you react to the teasing and what you do to correct your behavior is what will fix this over time. (Instructions can be provided here.) For example, some kids will call you "hyper" because they know that this hurts your feelings and then you will lose your temper and get into trouble. They even laugh when this happens. If you were to ignore and not react to them, they would stop their little game of having fun at your expense. Keep in mind that you will have to follow this plan for a long time before they change how they react to you. Remember, you have a certain reputation with them. They expect that if they keep it up, you'll overreact. So it won't be easy to change them. With effort, however, you could do it and succeed. Imagine how proud you will feel, when you beat them at their own game because you controlled yourself.

(CP6) I shouldn't have to be on a point system (a behavior modification program). It's not my fault that I have ADHD. I shouldn't have to purchase my privileges. These should be given to me because I am a child. Giving me what I want shows that people care about and love me.

(P6) Being on a point system doesn't mean that your parents and teachers are against you. On the contrary! Setting up and carrying out a point system is time consuming and hard work. It means that everyone has to be always ready to help you. The point system can teach you to concentrate and to make good choices. If you cooperate, not only will you be able to earn some neat things, but you will acquire better self-control. You will then be proud of yourself because you will be solving your own problems.

Although the preceding applies specifically to ADHD children, there are other negative views that young people hold which interfere with their capacity to function successfully. This author (Lavin,1991) has identifies a number of "twisted" thoughts, which if replaced with "straight" thinking, can also help ADHD children to gain better control of their emotions and behavior. With regard to PC6, the use of behavior modification in conjunction with cognitive restructuring can be particularly efficacious in teaching the ADHD child to attend, to control impulsivity, and to take responsibility for making better choices. Behavior modification, in combination with other treatment modalities, has been highly recommended by researchers and practitioners who work with the ADHD population (Barkley, 1990; Byrd & Byrd, 1986; Gomez & Cole, 1991; Lavin, 1991; McGuiness, 1985).

# X. USING COGNITIVE RESTRUCTURING TO TEACH IMPULSE CONTROL AND PERSISTENCE

Cognitive restructuring, as indicated previously, provides the basic structure upon which a healthy self-concept is built. By positively and realistically altering negative thinking, a foundation for helping the ADHD child to acquire better impulse control is laid. Teaching self-control is probably one of the most difficult tasks undertaken by those caregivers who work with ADHD children. Self-control requires two things. First, the child must be able to avoid giving into the temptation of avoiding responsibility. Second, the child must be able to structure his or her time, energy, and resources to satisfactorily complete assigned tasks within reasonable time limits. If we examine the characteristics of successfully achieving youngsters, we will usually find that they have enough self-control to complete their schoolwork and chores at home on time. Thus, they do not have to make excuses for not getting things done. Further, usually such children do more than the required minimum. This results in a quality of performance far above the mediocrity with which their peers are often satisfied. Most importantly, these youngsters are able to maintain control over themselves and the use of their time. For example, they control how much TV that they watch. By sensibly budgeting their TV viewing, they leave enough time to complete more important responsibilities. This same control is exercised in other areas of life as well. For instance, the amount of time spent in reading, talking on the telephone, playing with friends, and so forth is allotted on a sensible, priority basis. Thus, the lives of these children are usually well-ordered and goal directed. As a result, they avoid the excuses used by their less self-disciplined peers.

**Teaching good impulse control**

In teaching the ADHD child to control him or herself, the importance of the "self" must first be emphasized. The caregiver must help the child to understand that the self has three parts: (1) intellectual, (2) emotional, and (3) behavioral. We must then show the child how each of these contributes to his or her total functioning as a person. We have found it helpful to begin with a simple lesson in physiology. First, with regard to the intellectual and behavioral parts, we usually begin by talking about the brain. For example, we might ask the child to move his or her right hand. Next, we ask how he or she did this. Then we discuss how the brain sent a message to the hand telling it to move. We point out that the brain is the focal point of the body. It directs behavior by telling the arms, legs, or mouth what or what not to do.

To make this lesson even clearer, an illustration might be provided by drawing an outline of the brain with buttons. We then explain that pushing one of these buttons transmits messages through the nervous system to the various body parts. These messages direct our actions. We might then ask the youngster to engage in a few more behaviors such as standing, sitting, putting the right hand on the left arm, and so forth. We continue to discuss how the communication sent from the brain to the body parts resulted in certain behaviors. We also point out that the child may decide not to do these things. The brain might transmit a message such as, "The teacher wants me to put my left hand on my head. That is foolish and I refuse to do it." Thus, despite the teacher's directive, this self-talk would result in the youngster doing something else or nothing at all. The critical point in this simple lesson is that the child has the control. By thinking correctly or by pushing the proper "brain buttons," the child can make him or herself do or not do certain things. Hence, the rudiments of self-control are taught. This example teaches children that they can cause their own behavior.

In discussing the emotional aspect of impulse control, a similar approach is used. We begin by teaching "feeling words," labels to identify specific emotions. It is important that the child learn to distinguish between a feeling word and an opinion. Sometimes we make statements such as, "I feel like going to the movies," or "I feel that what he did was unfair." Such statements are not feeling words. They are opinions or expressions of what we want. Feeling words, on the other hand, convey our emotional reactions. These are words such as "anger," "anxious," "depressed," "happy," and so forth. It is helpful to make a list of such words with the child and discuss the differences between them. This can be done by focusing on the behavioral manifestations of each emotion. For example, in discussing "anxiety," you can point out that trembling, looking down, hand twisting, and blushing often occur when we are anxious. Also, you and the child might make a list of feeling words on a chart. The youngster might then cut out pictures from magazines to match them.

Once the child is knowledgeable about emotions, it would be helpful to go back to the earlier discussion of the brain. The caregiver can now show how the messages from the brain influence our feelings about ourselves. For example, as noted in the previous chapter, there are a number of messages the brain could deliver that would cause the child to become discouraged. Such messages undermine the child's confidence and interfere with his or her ability to overcome challenges. The following are examples of such self-defeating messages: (1) I am stupid; (2) I always make mistakes; (3) There is no use trying because I'll fail anyway; and (4) I might as well avoid work and have fun now because I'll mess up no matter how hard I try. Obviously, if these "brain buttons" are repeatedly pushed, they will have a direct impact on how the child feels about him or herself. In other words, constant repetition of such self-statements will result in feelings of discouragement, depression, or self-pity. This occurs because the child believes that he or she is incapable of being successful. Naturally, with such a view of self, the youngster would be more likely to watch TV than do homework. In addition, such a child would avoid responsibilities and be more concerned with having fun. In fact, the research on child development supports this (Fry, 1975).

We know that a child's immediate emotional state influences his or her ability to resist temptation and to maintain self-control. If a child is depressed, then he or she is more likely to give up rather than persist when challenged. On the other hand, if a child is happy and optimistic, there is a greater likelihood that he or she will continue to try to be successful. Thus, it is important to emphasize that there is a direct connection between what children learn to say about themselves and how they feel and behave. If a youngster repeatedly makes statements such as "I am dumb;" "I can't do it;" or "I'll probably mess up," he or she will feel depressed much of the time. Such a child will then behave like a discouraged person. This means that the youngster will put off or avoid engaging in challenging tasks. In addition, the youngster will often whine and fuss when confronted with difficulty. This will be followed by excuses such as "I didn't have time" when responsibilities are not completed. If we want children to acquire good self-control, it is important to teach them to alter their mood states. This can be done by teaching them to replace counterproductive thinking with sensible thoughts about their ability to perform successfully. Positive, realistic thoughts such as the following should be stressed: (1) If I try, there is always a chance that I can be successful. If I quit, there is no chance; (2) I am capable of doing what is required of me if I am willing to make the effort: (3) I can meet my responsibilities if I really want to; and (4) I'm just like other people. I'm good at some things and I have difficulty with others. Note that these statements are realistic, rather than grandiose. Making statements such as "I'm great" or "I'm better than other people" are usually exaggerations. These can easily lead to self-centeredness and arrogance. In fact, many people who make such statements about themselves exaggerate in order to cover up their own sense of insecurity. Thus, it is important to teach the child to make self-statements that are both realistic and positive. Discouragement and depression can then be replaced with feelings of hope and confidence. This, in turn, leads to productive behaviors that enable the child to achieve successfully. The child who thinks, feels, and behaves positively will receive good feedback from other people. This reinforces the positive feelings the child has about him or herself. Further, it makes it even more likely that he or she will display better self-control in the future.

It is important to actually instruct the child in realistic, positive thinking. This will help the youngster to control his or her feelings and behavior. The research on child development shows that teaching children to generate their own verbal instructions for coping with situations requiring self-control can be beneficial even at the preschool level (Fry, 1975; Hartig & Kanfer, 1973). We all know that children are placed in a variety of situations in which there is great temptation to avoid responsibility. For example, the temptation to watch TV instead of doing homework is a common problem which most parents face. Thus, it is essential to provide the youngster with instructions on how to cope with the impulse to avoid this responsibility. First, parents must identify with the child those situations most likely to cause difficulty. They might then discuss the pluses and minuses of doing and not doing the work. The following technique can be helpful in this regard. Take a sheet of paper and draw a line down the middle. Place a plus sign over one column and a minus sign over the other. The parents and child can then list all of the pros and cons in each of the respective columns. A sensible examination of the pluses and minuses associated with each choice can then be made.

Following the preceding, the child can be taught specific statements that can enhance his or her ability to begin and to stay on task. For example, when the youngster comes home from school with assignments, the temptation to watch TV is a real problem. Thus, after identifying this situation as potential trouble, the following verbal instructions might be taught to the child: "As soon as I get into the house, I will immediately go to my room and begin my homework. I will do it neatly and accurately and not allow myself to be distracted by the TV. If I do this, I will be showing good self-control. This will please me and my parents." Note that in these statements, the verbal instructions emphasize when and what will be done ("As soon as I get into the house, I will go immediately to my room and begin my homework."), the temptation to be avoided ("and not let myself to be distracted by the TV"), and the consequences for controlling oneself ("I will be showing good self-control. This will please me and my parents."). These statements should help the child to initiate and maintain his or her self-control.

For younger children of preschool or early elementary school age, the sentences should be shortened to help them to retain the information. For example, let's suppose that the cookie jar is full of freshly baked cookies. You do not want your child to take the cookies without permission because eating them interferes with what he or she consumes at meal time. The following verbal instructions might then be taught to the child: "I am not going to take cookies from the cookie jar when I see it. I will be good and Mommy and Daddy will be proud of me." Note that these statements indicate what the child is going to do and when it is going to be done. Further, the consequences for behaving appropriately are specified. The preceding examples provide the youngster with a verbal strategy for coping with potentially stressful situations. In fact, this approach can be applied successfully with a number of situations requiring good self-control.

# XI. SELF-CONTROL GAMES FOR ADHD CHILDREN

While cognitive restructuring is a critical component in helping the ADHD child in controlling impulsivity, it is also important for the youngster to become more cognizant of how he or she typically behaves. Such knowledge is called "objective self-awareness" (Liebert & Nelson, 1981). In order to increase the child's objective awareness, it is helpful to distinguish between good and poor self-control. This can be done by using games that teach the child to focus on his or her behavior. For instance, presenting the child with a frustrating task such as untying a knotted shoestring or putting together a difficult puzzle can be helpful in this regard. Such a task is potentially frustrating because a prize can be earned if it is successfully completed within a short time limit. As the child is attempting the task, describing what he or she is doing that shows good and poor problem solving can be presented. For instance, the child might demonstrate poor frustration control by repeating the same errors again and again. The parent might say, "You are getting frustrated because you are making the same mistakes again and again. Take a deep breath and calm yourself. Now try a different way to solve the problem. Good! You are putting the blue puzzle parts together and matching them with the green parts. Now you are making progress." By using this approach, a teacher or parent can assist the child in three ways. First, they can help the child to label the emotion that is interfering with his or her ability to think. Second, they can point out the inappropriate behavior causing the failure. Third, they can identify the problem solving strategies that are most likely to be successful. When the problem is completed, parents or teachers can specifically distinguish between those behaviors that show good and poor frustration control. Such a technique increases the youngster's awareness of self. Moreover, it teaches the child to put good behavioral strategies into practice for coping with future situations.

In order to enhance the ADHD child's capabilities to concentrate and acquire better self-control, we have put together a manual entitled SELF-

CONTROL TRAINING GAMES FOR CHILDREN. The manual focuses on exercises that parents, teachers, and mental health professionals can use to help ADHD children to gain greater "objective self-awareness" leading to improved impulse control and coping skills. This manual, which follows, has been reproduced in its entirety so that these games can be put into practice by those who are responsible for rearing and educating our ADHD children.

# SELF-CONTROL TRAINING GAMES FOR CHILDREN

Paul Lavin Ph.D.

# TABLE OF CONTENTS

# INTRODUCTION

*Training young minds not to wander: New research suggests that, beyond genes, experience affects specific brain network involved in attention.* The preceding is the caption of an article written by Bridget Murray in the October 2003 *Monitor* published by the American Psychological Association. The article describes the work of Dr. Michael Posner, a professor emeritus of cognitive psychology at the University of Oregon. Dr. Posner is currently conducting cutting edge research, the preliminary results of which show that children can improve attention efficiency by engaging in daily training exercises specifically designed to achieve this objective. According to Dr. Posner, attention-training exercises facilitate the development of neural networks in the human brain. This is particularly important for children because such networks are still forming. Such malleability makes them good candidates for profiting from this training.

Posner points out that there are three major components to understanding how attention develops. These are: (1) maintaining alertness or focus; (2) orienting to visual and auditory stimuli; and (3) sustaining executive or voluntary control or suppressing competing cognitions or emotions to complete a task. According to Posner, "We should think of this work (attention-training) not just as remediation but as a normal part of education. Attention plays a very important role in the acquisition of high-level skills, and if attention is trainable, it becomes attractive for preschool preparation."

For twenty-five years, Norbel School has been educating children diagnosed with attention deficit hyperactivity disorder (ADHD) and learning disabilities. We have long been aware of the fact that the ability to sustain concentration was not only essential in acquiring academic competence, but that this skill was also critical in helping children to learn to control their thinking, emotions, and behavior. This has been part of our educational package throughout Norbel School's history. As we all know, the formation of good habits does not occur by chance. Rather, the child must be trained to focus upon and sustain a concentrated effort in building those skills and character traits that will enable him or her to cope successfully with life's challenges.

The training exercises presented in this booklet have been developed with the preceding purpose in mind. They have been designed to teach the child to focus and stay on task. Moreover, the child is required to attend to those internal and external stimuli necessary for performing successfully. The "blocking out" and/or modifying of potentially competing environmental and emotional factors that could interfere with his or her performance is required as well.

By participating in these exercises or games, the child is being taught to concentrate and to develop those cognitive and behavioral skills, which facilitate the acquisition of good self-control. It is our contention that children can be trained to bring this about. The games presented in this booklet are a "fun way" to assist our youngsters to achieve this objective. Hopefully, parents, educators, and mental health professionals will find these to be of benefit in working with their children.

## TEACHING SELF-CONTROL

1. What is self-control?

Self-control is a person's ability to regulate his or her actions.

2. What is good self-control?

Persons with good self-control are able to do the following: (1) think before they act, (2) identify the most efficacious solutions for solving problems, and (3) perform those actions necessary for bringing the problem to a satisfactory resolution.

3. How is good self-control acquired?

Acquiring good self-control is a learned skill. In order to acquire good self-control, learning how to manage our bodies, minds, and behavior is necessary.

## 4. How do we begin to learn self-control?

We begin to learn self-control by starting with our bodies. Our bodies are made up of many parts which function separately and in coordination with one another. The "control tower" or "power source" which directs the movement of these parts is the brain. The brain does this by dictating messages to each body part. These messages travel through wires extending from the brain to each part of the body. The wires are called the nervous system. They carry the messages from the brain telling each body part how it is supposed to behave. The messages may tell the body part to remain stationary or to move with varying degrees of intensity.

## 5. How do we prepare our children to learn about self-control?

First, we need to prepare a large diagram of the human body showing the brain, nervous system, and body parts. The diagram should be simple, containing the head, the torso, and the extremities (hands, feet, legs, arms etc.). The nervous system or "connecting wires" from the brain to the various body parts should be clearly presented in the diagram. The following can then be presented:

"Who knows what this is?" (Wait for a student to respond with "The human body." If no person gives a correct response, indicate that this is a picture of the human body and its parts. If a student responds correctly, continue with the lesson.) "That's right. It is a picture of the human body. Let's look at the picture and identify the different body parts." (Point to each part and label it. Leave the brain and the nervous system until the end of the lesson.)

"Now we have identified the hands, legs, feet, arms, etc. What is this part called?" (Point to the brain. Wait for the correct response. If it is not forthcoming, identify the brain. If the correct answer is given, continue as follows.) "That's right. It is called the brain. Who can tell me what the brain does? Who can tell me why the brain is so important?" (Wait for a response. If there is no satisfactory response say, "The brain thinks." If a student responds correctly, then continue with the lesson.)

"That's correct. The brain thinks. The brain actually tells us what to do and how we should do it. It tells each part of the body how it wants it to behave. For example, everyone hold up their right hand. Now shake your hand back and forth like this." (Demonstrate and have the children copy you.) "Good. Everyone is shaking their hand back and forth. Now stop." (Wait until everyone has ceased shaking his or her hand.) "Who can answer this question? What part of your body told you to shake your right hand and then to stop?" (Wait for the correct response or state "The brain," if no answer is given. If a correct answer occurs, continue as follows.)

"Correct. Your brain said to you, 'Shake your right hand back and forth. Now stop.' It was your brain that told you how to behave. Your brain said 'Shake' and 'Stop.' It controlled what you did." (Once this is understood, continue as follows.)

"You can see how the brain works. It tells us what it wants each part of our body to do and we then follow its directions. Now I want you to look at these lines that connect the brain with each of the body parts." (Point to each of these and trace the connection from the brain to the body parts.) "These lines are called the nervous system. These are like telephone wires that connect the speaker and the listener to each other. The lines or wires of the nervous system carry the words or messages from the speaker, which is the brain, to the body part, which is the listener. In other words, the wires of the nervous system deliver the message from the brain to each body part telling it what it wants it to do." (Once the children grasp this concept, summarize the lesson as follows.)

"Now let's review what we have learned today. Our bodies are made up of different parts. It is our brain, however, that tells or directs these parts on how to behave. It is our brain that tells us to shake a hand, point a finger, or kick a ball. And it is our brain that tells us to sit still, to stand straight, or to not to do anything. Our nervous system consists of wires that connect the brain to the different parts of the body. These wires carry the messages from the brain to each body part telling it how to behave. Who could tell me what would happen if the brain became damaged or destroyed?" (Wait for the correct response. If this is not forthcoming, supply the correct answer. If the answer is given, continue as follows.)

"That's right. The body would be unable to control its movements because no messages could be given telling it what to do. What would happen if the wires connecting the brain and the body were cut or destroyed?" (Use same procedure as in the preceding paragraph.) "Correct. Even though the brain told the body what to do, the messages would not get delivered to the parts. So the body would not be able to behave as it is supposed to. For example, you all know what happens when a storm knocks out or breaks our power lines. Even though your telephone, television, lights, stove, and refrigerator are not damaged, they cannot work because the power or the messages that make them work are not getting there. Does anyone have any questions about the material that we have covered?" (Conclude at this point.)

## SELF-CONTROL TRAINING EXERCISES: WHAT ARE THEY?

1. What are self-control training exercises?

Self-control training exercises are games that we play in order to learn how to control our bodies, minds, and behavior. Self-control games require that we do the following: (1) focus attention on the trainer, (2) listen to the trainer's instructions, (3) repeat the instructions to ourselves so that we can remember them, (4) continue to concentrate on the instructions while playing the game so that becoming distracted does not interfere with our performance, and (5) performing the appropriate actions needed to successfully participate in the game.

2. What do self-control games teach us to do?

Self-control games teach us to use our brain to control our body, mind, feelings, and actions. We learn to use "self-talk" in order to regulate what we do and say. Self-talk consists of saying words, phrases, and sentences to ourselves in our head. These verbal messages, which are delivered by our brain to the various parts of our body, help us to concentrate on the task at hand and to satisfactorily complete it. Self-control games teach us that we, not outside events, other people, or fate, determine what happens to us.

## SELF-CONTROL TRAINING GAMES

### The "Be Quiet" Game

The purpose of the Be Quiet game is to teach children to refrain from speaking impulsively. Children learn that they can choose to speak or to remain silent by focusing and selectively ignoring distractions which are designed to take them off task. The Be Quiet game teaches the child that he or she has control over his or her mouth and the sounds and speech that come from it. The following instructions can be given to the children in introducing this game:

"Today we are going to play a game called the Be Quiet game. I want to see how many people can keep from uttering a single sound or word when I try to trick them into speaking. Here is how the game works. You are supposed to sit quietly while the game is being played. Do not make a sound or say a word. For each minute that you stay silent, you will earn (e.g. a chip, token, point, extra minute at recess etc.). While you are being silent, I am going to try to trick you into talking with me. I will ask you questions, make comments, and try to get you to make a sound or a comment. If you get tricked, then I will take away any rewards that you have earned, and you will have to start over. The longer that you can remain silent while I am trying to trick you, the more rewards you can earn. If anyone goes the entire time (e.g. 10 minutes) without making a sound or saying a word, he or she will receive a bonus of (specify the extra reward). Let's begin by sitting upright in our chairs. Now look directly at me. Are there any questions? (Answer questions.) Okay. Let's get ready. Begin now!" (A kitchen or egg timer might be used so that the children can observe the passing of time.)

While the time is passing, the following can be said by the instructor:

"Everyone is silent so far. Everyone is in control of his or her mouth. Nobody has been tricked or distracted yet. Let's see if I can trick some people. Christine, that's a nice dress that you are wearing. What color is it?" (If Christine responds, point out that you tricked her, and the goal of the game is to be silent. Remove any rewards and encourage her to start over and not get tricked a second time. If Christine remains silent, continue as follows.) "Good, Christine! You did not get tricked or distracted. Your brain told you to keep your mouth closed and not to answer." (Reward Christine accordingly. Proceed in the same manner in trying to "trick" other children. Make similar comments when they succeed or fail.)

When the exercise is completed, identify those who have successfully avoided being tricked by your distractions. Give bonus rewards. Discuss how they prevented themselves from being tricked into speaking. Questions such as the following can be addressed:

1. What did you say to yourself to keep from being tricked? How was that helpful?

2. What did you say to yourself while I was trying to trick you?

3. How did you stay focused on the rewards that you could earn?

4. How did you feel when you could successfully control yourself? What did you think or say to yourself?

5. What did you learn from playing this game?

## The "No-Wiggle" Game

The purpose of the No-Wiggle game is to teach children that they can control their body parts, stay within their own personal space, and avoid intruding into the personal space of their peers. The No-Wiggle game focuses on teaching the child to be fully aware of his or her body parts and his or her ability to coordinate and control them.

To begin the game have the children sit in a hardback chair with feet flat on the floor, their shoulders and back against the chair, their head centered and upright (no slouching), and their hands flat on their thighs. Once each child is in the proper position, reinforce him or her with a chip, token, points, or some other reward. The following instructions can then be given:

"Today we are going to focus on controlling all of our body parts together. All of you are now sitting upright, quietly, and have full control of your entire body. I want you to remain in this position. There is to be no wiggling, moving about, or changing your position. You must sit with your feet flat on the floor, your back and shoulders against the chair, your head centered and upright, and your hands flat on your legs. For every thirty seconds that you hold this position without any wiggling whatsoever, you will receive a reward of (e.g. chips, tokens, points, extra recess time, etc.) The longer that you keep from wiggling, the more rewards you will receive. If you go the entire time (5 to 10 minutes) without any movement, you will receive a bonus of (specify the extra reward for a perfect performance). If you are caught wiggling, not matter how small a movement you might make, then the rewards that you have earned will be taken away. At this point, you must start over."

Before actually starting the game, let the children relax their bodies for about a minute. Answer any questions that might arise pertaining to the game's purpose and how it is to be played. Then continue, "Okay. Sit in your chair and put your head, back and shoulders, feet, and hands in the proper position." (Make sure each child is seated properly. Make corrections if needed.) A timer might be set and placed accordingly so that the children can observe the passage of time while the game is being played. Following this state, "Get ready. Begin now!"

While the children are seated, the following can be stated by the instructor as he or she moves about the room. "I like the way that you are showing good self-control. Your hands are flat on your thighs and are still. Your head is upright and centered. Your back and shoulders are against the chair, and you are sitting in a straight position. All of your body parts are working together and are in total control. There is no wiggling. You are the boss of your body parts. Your brain is telling all of your body parts to be stationary and that no wiggling is allowed. Your body parts are following your brain's instructions."

When the time for the game has ended, dispense the bonus rewards to those who have maintained the No-Wiggle position throughout this exercise. A discussion focusing on the following questions might then be undertaken:

1. What did you say to yourself to keep from wiggling?

2. What did it feel like trying to keep your body in control?

3. What was the most difficult part of playing this game? Why? How did you cope with this?

4. How did you feel when you were successful in keeping yourself in control? Why?

5. What did you learn from playing this game?

## The "Mini-Movement" Game

The purpose of this game is to teach the child greater body control than that required in the No-Wiggle game. This exercise requires that the child deliver instructions to the various body parts telling them to behave in opposition to each other. Like the No-Wiggle game, the youngster is required to hold his or her body in a stationary position. However, he or she is then asked to move a specific body part(s) while the remaining parts are held in check. For example, the trainer might ask the children to lift their right hand and to repeatedly tap on their right thigh. While they are engaging in this behavior, all other body parts must continue to be held in a stationary position. This game could be made even more challenging by having the children repeatedly rub their stomachs with their left hand in conjunction with the tapping of their thigh by the right hand. Again, the other body parts must remain rigid while these two actions are taking place. Adding different movements of more body parts increases the difficulty of this exercise. Obviously, the more challenging the task, the greater is the self-control that is required. Variations of this game might include alternately the right and left hands on each thigh, tapping the top of the head with one hand and rubbing the stomach with the other hand, alternately tapping the right and left foot on the floor, etc. Different and more challenging combinations can be devised at the trainer's discretion.

In introducing this game, the directions describing the No-Wiggle game can be used. The children would be told to keep their body parts in a rigid position except for the one, two, or more parts that were to be engaged in some particular motion. Once this is demonstrated and explained, the game can begin. Like all of the preceding games, rewards would be dispensed at specific time intervals, and a bonus reward would be given to those children who were successful for the entire experience. The following patter could be used while the children are playing the game:

"Remember, you must keep your body in check. However, at the same time, you must continue to tap your right hand on your right thigh. Keep you head centered and upright. Keep your back and shoulders against the chair. Keep your feet flat on the floor. Keep your left hand flat on your left thigh. But remember to keep that right hand tapping on your right thigh."

Continue with the preceding patter until the game is finished. Bonus rewards can then be distributed. At the conclusion of the game, the following questions might be addressed:

1. How was this game different from the No-Wiggle game?
2. Which game is harder? Why?
3. What did you have to do to be successful in this game?
4. Does this game require greater self-control? Why or why not?
5. What did you learn from playing this game?

**The "Controlled Rocking Chair" Game**

This game is designed for children who have mastered their bodies by successfully participating in the preceding exercises. They are now ready to engage in games requiring that they use their bodies to control external stimuli as well. In order to do this exercise, a ball made out of crumpled newspaper or a paper bag is needed. The shape of the ball can be maintained by putting rubber bands around it. The surface of the ball will contain crumpled ridges which are needed to hold the ball on the arm of the chair. Also, a rocking chair with an arm of approximately six inches across will be needed. The ball is then placed on the arm of the chair. The surface of the ball should be rough enough to hold it on the arm but smooth enough so that excessive movement will cause it to fall.

The child is first taught to sit properly in the chair. The ball is then placed on the arm of the chair, and the child is told to rock the chair so that the ball falls off onto the floor. Following this, the ball is placed back onto the chair. The child is now instructed to gently rock the chair so that the ball stays on the arm. Once this is successfully accomplished, the child is asked to contrast movements that kept the ball on the chair with movements that caused it to fall. You might then state, "When you rock the chair in a quick, hard and careless fashion, the ball falls onto the floor. However, when you rock gently and carefully, the ball doesn't move and stays on the arm."

Once the preceding is completed, the game can be explained as follows: "The purpose of this game is to see if you can keep the ball on the arm of the chair while you are rocking it. Remember, if you rock too hard, the ball will fall. You must rock the chair carefully enough so that the ball stays on the arm for as long as possible. For every 30 seconds that you are able to keep the ball from falling, you will earn (specify a reward). If you are able to keep the ball on the arm of the chair for the full time (specify time limit of game, perhaps 5 minutes), you will receive a bonus of (specify bonus reward). In order to receive the rewards, you must keep the chair rocking throughout the game. If the ball falls or if you stop rocking the chair, you will lose the rewards you have earned and you must begin again. Are there any questions?" Answer questions. The game can then begin.

During the game, the following patter might be used by the trainer to encourage the child: "Excellent. You are continuing to rock the chair but the ball is staying on the arm. You are concentrating on the ball but your arms, legs, and body are moving just enough to keep the ball in position. Good concentration. Good controlled movements." At the conclusion of the exercise, the following questions might be addressed:

1. How was this different from the other games?
2. Why was this more difficult?
3. What did you have to be able to do to perform successfully?
4. What did you say to yourself that helped you to concentrate?
5. What did you learn from playing this game?

A variation of this game can be played by having the ball placed on the top of the back of the chair where the child cannot see it (a recliner chair has a back big enough to accommodate this). The child then sits in the same manner as he or she did in the preceding exercise. The child must now rock the chair and keep the ball from falling on to the floor without seeing it. He or she, therefore, must rely on his or her kinesthetic sense to successfully play this game. The following pattern might be used by the trainer:

"The ball is in position on the back of the chair even though you cannot see it. You are rocking the chair well—not too much but enough to keep the game going. Your hands, feet, and body are well controlled. The ball is still in position while you are continuing to rock."

Again, the same timing and reward system can be used as in the preceding exercise. Some discussion questions that might be asked at the conclusion are:

1. How was this different from the other rocking chair game?
2. What did you have to think about to be successful?
3. What did you learn from this exercise?

### The "Freeze" Game

The purpose of this game is to teach the child to bring his or her body under immediate control when directions are given to do so. This requires that the child, while engaging in full body motion, attend and respond to a command given by the trainer.

Before beginning this exercise, have the child (or children if this is a group) walk or march in a circle, moving his or her arms, legs, and torso. Explain that you want him or her to engage in this behavior until you say, "Freeze." At this moment, the child is to stop moving and remain in the exact position that occurred when the command was given. The child must hold this position without moving. If the child holds the position successfully, rewards can be dispensed at 15, 20, or 30 second intervals. Failure to "freeze" or any body movement thereafter would result in no rewards or a loss of those which have been earned previously. Once the timed interval has passed (use a stopwatch to determine this), the trainer will say, "Melt." On this command, the child is to continue moving until another "freeze" directive is given. This game can be played for about 10 minutes. If the child completes the exercise without any errors, a bonus reward for "perfect self-control" can be provided. The following discussion questions can be addressed at the conclusion of this game:

1. What was difficult about playing this game? Why?
2. How did you feel while playing the game?
3. What did you say to yourself in trying to keep from moving when the command "freeze" was given?
4. What did you learn by playing this game?

### "My Circuits Are Overloaded" Game

The purpose of this game is to train the child to concentrate and complete tasks in the presence of competing auditory and visual stimuli which are designed to take him or her off-task. The successful completion of this game requires not only that the child finish an assigned task, but he or she must "block-out" and/or prevent him or herself from being distracted by these extraneous, contrived stimuli. A high degree of concentration, persistence, and sustained "on-task" behavior is needed to successfully play this game.

The game is explained to the child (or children if this is used with a group) as follows:

"Today we are going to play a game called the My Circuits Are Overloaded game. I am going to give you a worksheet with 15 arithmetic problems on it. These problems are simple enough to complete if you pay attention and work on them." (The problems should be geared to the child's appropriate educational level. They should be easy enough that they could be completed satisfactorily in ordinary, quiet circumstances. However, they should be sufficiently challenging to require a concentrated effort on the child's part.) "You will have (Pick a time interval, perhaps 10 to 15 minutes) to finish the assignment. However, while you are working, I am going to try to distract you. The television, computer or other types of potentially distracting visual stimuli will be turned on and the radio or television's voice volume will be turned up so that you can hear them. I will be walking around the room holding up pictures and talking in order to try and distract you. Your job will be to try and accurately complete all of the arithmetic problems while these distractions are occurring. This will not be easy. However, for every arithmetic problem that you satisfactorily complete, a reward (specify reward) will be given. If you complete all 15 problems successfully, you will receive a bonus of (specify reward). Are there any questions?" (Answer these and then continue.) "Remember. I am going to try to distract you from completing your work. You must prevent yourself from being tricked into paying attention to the distractions. You will have 15 minutes to complete the work. Get ready. Begin now!" Put all of the distractions into effect at this point.

At the conclusion of the game, the answers to the arithmetic problems can be given. A bonus reward can be provided to anyone who completed all items successfully. Some discussion questions that might be addressed are as follows:

1. Why was this a difficult game to play?

2. What did you have to be able to do to perform successfully?
3. What did you say to yourself to keep from being distracted?
4. What was the most difficult part of trying to complete the work?
5. What did you learn from playing this game?

## The "I Can Stand It" Game

The purpose of this game is to teach the child to concentrate and persist when confronted with challenges. To successfully play this game, the child must be able to tolerate and cope with frustration. Potentially frustrating tasks are designed to challenge the child. The youngster must learn how to keep his or her "cool" and use good planning skills in order to complete the task within a set time limit.

The materials to be used for these games would be puzzles, items requiring the assembling or disassembling of parts, or working one's way through a maze. The activities should not be intrinsically interesting, such as playing a video game. Rather, tasks, which by their very nature would be perceived to be uninteresting, boring, or frustrating to the child should be presented. The required activities would demand that the child be persistent and use good planning skills in solving the problem. For example, the trainer could tie knots in the child's shoes and require that the youngster undo them in two minutes. A valuable reward might be offered as an incentive for successful completion of the task. Or the child might be presented with a puzzle which must be completed in fifteen minutes. Again, a reward could be offered for successfully completing the task.

Before beginning these games, the trainer should discuss those behaviors that enhance and detract from good problem solving. For instance, whining, complaining, throwing a temper tantrum, and impulsively repeating the same errors take away from one's ability to perform successfully. On the other hand, remaining calm, reflecting on one's actions, trying different approaches, and persisting can lead to success.

The following can be stated in introducing the game to the child: "Today we are going to play the I Can Stand It game. I am going to give you this problem to solve. Here are several different colored fishing lines which are tangled together. What I would like you to do is to separate the lines. In other words, untangle them so that each line is separated from the others. This is not going to be an easy task. It will require that you be patient, work hard, and not become overly frustrated and give up. You will have to concentrate and try different ways to untangle the lines. I will give you 10 minutes to solve this problem. If you complete the task satisfactorily, you will earn (specify a reward). Do you understand what to do? (Answer questions and continue.) Okay. Get ready. Begin!" Use a stopwatch to time the task. Announce the time remaining at one minute intervals.

While the game is progressing, the following patter can be used to assist the child: "I like the way that you are examining and concentrating on the problem. It is good that you are trying different approaches to untangling the lines. Good concentration. Excellent self-control. That's the way to calm down. Taking a deep breath can be helpful. You are not letting frustration get the best of you. Good persistence. You are sticking to it and not letting it make you give up."

At the end of 10 minutes, stop the game. If the child has successfully solved the problem, the reward should be given. The following questions might be discussed:

1. What did you do that was helpful in working on the problem?
2. What did you do that interfered with helping you to solve the problem?
3. What could you have done better?
4. What could you say to yourself to help you to stay calm and not give up?
5. What did you learn from playing this game?

**The "Silly Instructions" Game**

The purpose of this game is to teach the child to listen and carry out one, two, or more instructions which are nonsensically connected to each other. This requires that the child concentrates, processes, and retains both simple and complex instructions. Moreover, performing the instructions in proper sequence is required.

The game is explained to the child as follows: "We are going to play a game to see how well you can remember and follow directions. I am going to give you some silly instructions. After I give these, I am going to ask you to repeat them back to me. If you can say them back to me in the right order, I will reward you with (specify reward). Following this, I will then ask you to perform these directions. If you do these in the correct order, you will receive another (specify reward). Do you have any questions? (Answer questions and then continue.) "Okay. Let's try a practice run before we begin. Remember, I will give you some silly instructions. You will then repeat them back to me. Following this, you are to carry out the directions. Now listen carefully. Pick up your pencil with your right hand. Put the pencil in your left hand. Then put the pencil on the table. Repeat this back to me." (If the child is successful, continue. If he or she is not successful, then review the directions until they are correctly stated.)

Once success occurs, say: "Good. Now carry out the directions." (If the child is unsuccessful, repeat the directions until they are followed correctly; once this occurs, the real game is ready to begin.)

A sample game using silly instructions is as follows: "Take the green book out of the book case. Put it under your right arm. Then place the book flat on the floor. Kneel on the book with your right knee." The trainer can easily devise other activities similar to the preceding. The instructions can require a single act or they can require several sequentially related behaviors depending on the child's level of ability.

In playing this game, it is best to begin by having the child repeat the directions out loud so that the trainer can hear them and make the appropriate corrections if needed. Following this, the required behaviors can be performed. Once the preceding has been mastered, the next step would be to simply have the youngster carry out the instructions without repeating them out loud. The trainer can suggest that the child say the directions to him or herself to facilitate remembering them. The two-step process is, therefore, now reduced to one step, which consists of just carrying out the "silly" instructions.

Rewards can be dispensed for successful performance. Again, the trainer can begin by rewarding the successful completion of simple one-step instructions. Greater rewards can be given for successfully following multiply complex steps as the child becomes increasingly more competent. The following discussion questions can be addressed at the conclusion of the game:

1. What makes this game so difficult?
2. What do you have to do to be successful?
3. What strategies can you use to help yourself?
4. How is this different from some of the other games?
5. What did you learn from playing this game?

# XII. USING CHILDREN'S STORIES TO TEACH GOOD PLANNING SKILLS

Helping the ADHD child to acquire good planning skills and better emotional controls is critical if he or she is to achieve successfully. Stories, fairy tales, and other forms of children's literature can be used to instruct youngsters in the principles of successful living. The advantage of using children's literature is that it appeals to the child's fantasy and imagination. Youngsters often identify with the characters portrayed in these stories, and there are a number of excellent stories and tales that parents can read to their children. Often these stories contain a moral emphasizing the importance of persistence, courage, and the willingness to confront hardships and challenges in the pursuit of noble goals.

For instance, all of us can remember the story, *The Tortoise and the Hare*. By being diligent and persistent, the tortoise won the race even though the odds were decidedly against him. How about the story, *The Little Engine That Could?* When confronted with climbing the steep and formidable hill, the little engine kept chugging along saying, "I think I can; I think I can; I think I can." The little engine kept repeating this message to himself. This increased his self-confidence and inspired him to overcome the challenge of the hill. If we think about it, the little engine was actually applying the self-instruction techniques discussed previously.

Another good story that teaches children the value of planning ahead is *The Little Red Hen*. As you might remember, it was the little red hen who planted the wheat, harvested it, and baked the bread. The goose, the cat, and the rat declined helping her and lazily frittered away their time. When the food was ready to eat, however, they received none. Doesn't a story like this convey the importance of using good judgment in preparation for the future?

As one can see, the messages contained in various children stories can be a valuable adjunct in helping ADHD youngsters to develop a responsible, productive attitude about life. It is important to keep in mind that children have vivid imaginations and love to use them. This can partly account for the success of many fast food products, toys, and breakfast cereals. The attractive, humorous characters associated with these products appeal to the child's sense of fantasy. Youngsters, therefore, want and even pressure their parents to purchase these products.

Younger children are more likely to identify with *The Little Engine That Could* or *The Tortoise and the Hare* while older children may be more likely to identify with sports, historical, or artistic heroes who have overcome challenges. The point to keep in mind is that young people are quite imaginative, fond of fantasy, and often identify with characters and people who have beat the odds in successfully coping with life's challenges. Parents and teachers can take advantage of this by reading stories that convey a moral relating to achievement and responsibility.

The following chapter (*Self-Control Stories for the ADHD Child*) includes original stories written with the ADHD child in mind. Each story addresses one or more characteristics of ADHD and includes after reading discussion points. In using these stories, remember to focus on each character's ability to change as well as the consequences of the character's actions. Encourage your child to identify a time when he or she felt similar to one or more of the characters. Discuss how he or she could have changed his or her behavior in order to deal with the situation more effectively.

## Guidelines for Using Children's Literature

The following guidelines can be helpful in using children's literature:

1. Familiarize yourself with various children's books at the school or local public library. Ask the librarian to help select stories stressing the importance of self-control, courage, persistence, and good judgment in coping with life's problems.

2. It is important to select books appropriate to the age and maturity level of the child. The librarian can also be helpful in this regard.

3. After selecting reading materials, choose a time when you and the child can sit quietly without interference from TV, playmates, or other

outside sources. It might be helpful to designate a "quiet time" during each day for the purpose of reading and talking together.

4.     Show the child the book and discuss the title and any illustrations on the cover. Ask the child what he or she thinks that the story will be about. This will stimulate the child's thinking and prepare him or her to anticipate what is about to happen.

5.     Involve the child by discussing pictures and how these relate to the story. Also, encourage the child to make predictions as to what will occur next in the story.

6.     As you are reading, be sure to accent and alter the tone of your voice when you come to key words, phrases, and dialogue. This will make the story more lifelike and interesting.

7.     When the story is completed, summarize the important events with the child. Discuss the main characters and how they behaved. This will help the child to make sense out of what was just read.

8.     After summarizing the story, discuss the lesson that was taught. Help the child to formulate a moral such as, "If you keep trying like the little engine and tell yourself that you can, you will be able to do it" or "If you keep trying like the turtle, you might win even though somebody thinks that they are better and can beat you."

9.     Once the moral is formulated, discuss how your child might use it in his or her life. You or the child might bring up specific situations in which the moral could be applied. For example, you might focus on how the child could be like the little engine when he or she has to complete a difficult school assignment. You might discuss how the youngster could be like the courageous lion in *The Wizard of Oz* when he or she has to face a challenge for the first time. By using the moral and helping the youngster to identify with the main character, he or she is being taught to incorporate the message in the story into his or her thinking.

One final point is important to keep in mind. In the preceding chapters, how to use points, stickers, and privileges to reward appropriate behavior was discussed. During the reading and discussion of a story, rewarding the child for sitting properly, listening, and "on-task" participation can be put into practice. While such incentives may not be needed, particularly if the child is interested in the material, these may be very helpful if the youngster has trouble sitting quietly and paying attention. Remember,

ADHD children respond best when a consistent and structured environment is provided. Thus, applying behavioral principles, even during story time (which should be intrinsically interesting), may be necessary in order to motivate them to participate viably in this activity.

# XIII. SELF-CONTROL STORIES FOR THE ADHD CHILD

Kathryn Lavin, M.A.

CHARLIE CHATTERBOX
THE PLUM SISTERS
AN UNCONTROLLABLE SNOUT
DRAGMALION

## CHARLIE CHATTERBOX

Charlie Chatterbox was always talking. In fact, he never, ever heard anyone ask him a question because he was too busy chatting. His teacher would constantly nag him, "Charlie Chatterbox, you are interrupting my lesson!" But did Charlie care? No way! He just kept talking, as if he was doing nothing wrong, making silly noises and poking his pencils together as if he was playing a video game. "Pencils in flight," he would cry, as his teacher was trying desperately to deliver a math lesson. Then, he would bang his pencils together, not listening to a word the teacher said.

One afternoon, a group of children decided to play "Duck, Duck, Goose." Charlie was talking to himself while the teacher was giving directions. When it was finally time for Charlie's turn to be the ducker, he had no idea what he was supposed to do. Instead of walking around the circle and tapping a goose on the head, Charlie ran into the middle of the circle screaming, "The duck is coming! The duck is coming!" Needless to say, Charlie's teacher sent him to stand at the wall for what he thought would be the rest of the game.

As he stood there talking to himself, Charlie began to grow more and more angry. "Everybody hates me!" he cried out. "I don't even want to play that stupid game anyway!" Then, he turned around and faced the wall. "I don't care about that game," he hollered as he buried his head in his hands. "I don't care about that stupid game...not one bit!"

For a few minutes, Charlie could hear the playful banter of the children behind him, the laughter, the excitement, and the giggling. Then, suddenly, the noises disappeared. At first he thought that the teacher was playing a trick on him. *She hates me anyway*, Charlie thought. But then after a few minutes of silence had passed, he decided that he should turn around just to be certain that he hadn't been left behind.

Sure enough, when Charlie turned around, he found himself all alone on the playground. "I knew they'd leave me!" he hollered. "I just knew it!" Hastily, he raced toward the front doors of the school building. But to his surprise, the doors had been bolted shut. "I knew it. I knew it. I knew it," Charlie chanted as he ran toward the classroom window. "I knew they'd lock me out!" He could see the children inside the classroom, sitting contently listening to the teacher's lesson. Immediately, he began rapping on the window. "Let me in!" he hollered. "Let me in!"

Losing control, Charlie reached back hoping to give the glass one final blow, when, suddenly, he was jolted up into the air.

A booming voice echoed from above: "Charlie Chatterbox, it is time that you see, how incredibly annoying your actions can be."

As his tiny little body dangled in the air, beams of lights flashed down around him. And when Charlie looked up, he noticed a giant silver ball emerging from the clouds. It looked like a spaceship.

"Goodbye, Ms. Meaniehead! Goodbye, meanie kids! Goodbye, stinky schoolwork, pitiful papers and crummy school lunches!" Charlie shouted, as he floated higher and higher into the sky.

Finally, he was free, free as a bird. It felt as if he were in a wonderful dream. But as everyone knows, dreams don't always come true, especially for someone like Charlie Chatterbox.

Just as the small boy floated past the fifth-grade window, an enormous hand reached down from the sky and snatched him abruptly. Charlie wriggled uncontrollably hoping to break free, but the hand was much too powerful for his petite seven-year-old body. The giant hand then pulled Charlie through a trap door and tossed him into a dark room filled with enormous television screens and lighted control panels.

Once again, Charlie heard a mysterious echo from above: "Charlie Chatterbox, it is time that you see, how incredibly annoying your actions can be."

Magically, images began to appear on the television screens. They were images of his second-grade classroom! As Charlie moved closer to the screens, he saw his classmates Jeanie Cooper, Mary Pat Parker, and Jason Clark. He saw his teacher Ms. Hillenbrand. And to his surprise, he saw himself!

Charlie jumped away from the screen and started to shout impulsively, "That's me! That's me!"

Then, he walked back toward the screens closer and closer, watching himself intently. He watched himself jump up and down on his chair in the middle of a math lesson. He watched himself flap his paper around during a test. He saw himself banging his pencils around in front of Martha McDonald's face. Then, he watched himself open up his pencil box and drop each of his pencils on the floor one, by one, by one.

For a moment, Charlie just sat there, stunned by what he had seen. He had never before seen himself act that way. It was just awful! He hung his head in shame.

But his self-pity was soon interrupted by a beam of light shooting down from the heavens. Once again, Charlie heard echoes from above: "Charlie Chatterbox, it is time that you see, how incredibly annoying your actions can be."

As the beams of light grew dimmer, Charlie noticed two enormous pencils standing before him. These two pencils were almost exactly like the pencils in his pencil box (except much bigger and much scarier looking). They even had "Property of Charlie Chatterbox" etched into the sides!

The first pencil stood straight up on its point and took one giant hop toward Charlie. "Is that him?" he asked.

The second pencil nodded. "That's him alright. The very boy who's been throwing us around for years, giving us eraser-ache, after eraser-ache, after eraser-ache!" It propped itself up on its hind eraser and pointed. "So, Charlie Chatterbox, tell me. What do you have to say for yourself?"

For once, Charlie was absolutely speechless.

"Speechless are you?" giggled the pencils "Speechless!"

The second pencil hopped forward. "We'll see how speechless you are when we pick *you* up and start banging *you* around!" Then, they started to move toward Charlie chanting, "People in Flight! People in Flight!"

There was nowhere to go! Nowhere to hide! Charlie Chatterbox was doomed! Fearing for his life, he threw his hands up over his eyes. Then, he waited…

And waited…

And waited…

And waited…

When, suddenly, he heard a most familiar voice. "Charlie Chatterbox! Charlie Chatterbox!"

He knew that voice! It was the voice of his teacher!

Finger by finger, Charlie uncovered his eyes and turned away from the wall. There before him, stood not only his teacher but all of his classmates.

"Charlie," giggled Ms. Hillenbrand, "you must have been in space. So," she continued, "we were wondering if you'd like another chance."

*Another chance*, thought Charlie. Another chance! Of course he wanted another chance. He had been saved!

Slowly, he walked over and joined the group. He sat down next to Martha McDonald, took a deep breath and smiled. He wasn't going to mess the game up for her. He owed it to her.

And at the end of the day, when recess was over, he went straight to his pencil box. He took out each pencil one by one and gently laid it back in his pencil box. Then, he took a deep breath, got into line, and for the first time walked out of school with the rest of his class...silently.

## Discussion Points

1.   In the beginning of the story, Charlie is told to take a time out. Do you believe that this was a fair consequence to his actions? Explain why or why not.

2.   In the beginning of the story, Charlie says that his teacher hates him. However, in the end of the story, she asks him if he would like to rejoin the game. Does this sound as if she hates him? Discuss how you think Charlie's teacher really feels about him.

3.   After Charlie sees himself on the television screen, he feels disappointed in himself. Identify reasons why he felt disappointed. What do you think he should do to make himself feel proud?

4.   When Charlie meets the pencils, they treat him in an unfriendly way. Give two reasons why the pencils treated him this way.

5.   Throughout the story, a voice from above echoes, "Charlie Chatterbox, it is time that you see how incredibly annoying your actions can be." Identify the actions the voice is talking about. Although we know that Charlie does not mean to be annoying, how are his actions annoying others?

6.   Tell about a way that Charlie could stay controlled while performing these actions.

7.   In the end, Charlie promises himself that he will try to do better. What can he do to help himself maintain control?

## Analysis

As the story indicates, Charlie's lack of control creates a problem for him, his teacher, and his classmates. Because Charlie is constantly talking or playing with his pencil box, he misses pivotal information, thereby affecting his behavior. When playing Duck, Duck, Goose, Charlie neglected to pay attention. As a result, he not only embarrassed himself but ended up in time-out for a large portion of the game. While in time-out, he complained, blaming the consequence on his teacher, rather than his actions.

Because he was constantly distracted, Charlie never noticed that his actions were problematic for others. He only became aware of this when forced to watch himself on the television screen. He then realized that his actions were in fact "annoying." After analyzing his behaviors, he rejoined the game with a new attitude.

In analyzing the story, an attempt must be made to discuss Charlie's behaviors and how these behaviors affect his relationship with his teacher and classmates. Explain that while Charlie does not mean to be hurtful, his actions create problems for others. Encourage the child to make suggestions as to how Charlie can control his behaviors, focusing on his ability and desire to change.

## THE PLUM SISTERS

Patty and Peggy Plum were born in the very same hospital, in the very same room, on the very same day. When the nurses saw them they squealed with delight, "They are even prettier than the Pinkerstown prom queen!" The doctors, of course, agreed, saying that Peggy and Patty Plum were the two most adorable girls to ever come out of the Pinkerstown Hospital.

From that day on, Mrs. Plum insisted that the two girls look exactly alike. "A perfectly placed pigtail with a perfectly placed bow is extremely important," she uttered. "And," she added, "all girls must look perfectly proper before entering the school building."

By the time breakfast was served, you could hardly tell the two girls apart. They looked perfectly prim and perfectly proper. But by the time they arrived at school, things looked different...very different.

When Mrs. Plum closed the front door, the two girls scrambled off on their separate ways. Patty would run off to play in the creek next to the old Farmer Harris' barnyard. She would wade in the stream, run after crayfish and hurl mud at the ancient oak trees. "Hee-yaa!" she would holler as she sent the mud flying through the air. Then, after about twenty minutes of mud slinging, she'd realize that she was late for school.

Peggy, on the other hand, walked directly to school. She knew that she must be there on time, dressed properly and ready to learn.

While everyone knew that the two girls were so very different, many did not know that in one particular way they were incredibly similar. Both of the girls had a gift. In the middle of the night, they were blessed with visions...visions of the future. A kind fairy would come to them, dressed in a blue diamond dress, wave her wand and whisper these words: "Peggy and Patty Prim and Proper Plum, it is because of you that I have come." Then she would give them important information about the future.

One evening, while fast asleep, the fairy came to the girls in their dreams. This time she was dressed in a velvet red gown with gold shimmers scattered along the seams.

"Peggy and Patty Prim and Proper Plum, it is because of you that I have come.

126

"Tomorrow," she whispered, "Is a monumental day,
You must wake early and be on you way,
For, outside of town, by the Untimely River,
Is something so cold it makes mammoths shiver,
Follow the path and mind what you do,
And a mountain of ice cream will be waiting for you."

And with that the good fairy vanished into thin air as quickly as she had come.

The very next morning, Patty awoke at the crack of dawn. "Ice cream!" she cried. "Ice cream!" She could hardly wait. Immediately, she shot out of bed, raced out the door, and began sprinting toward the Untimely River...dressed in her pajamas.

Peggy, of course, sat on her bed and reminded herself of what the good fairy had said. She carefully chose a snowsuit from her closet and paired it with a fur-lined fedora. Then, she slipped on her snow boots and began walking toward the Untimely River.

After what seemed to be hours, Patty discovered a fork in the road. She tried desperately to figure out which road would lead her to the mountain of ice cream. Then, suddenly she heard whispering from above.

"Patty Prim and Proper Plum, the good fairy told me that you may come."

She glanced up into the trees and saw a slick gray-haired possum staring down at her. The possum began speaking slowly and quietly.

"You may be wondering which direction to go,
Solve this riddle and then you will know,
Think carefully, think clearly. You must use your brain—"

"I can't take it anymore," Patty interrupted. "You are way too slow! I got people to meet, places to go! I don't have the time to sit here and diddle! You take the time to solve your old riddle!" And with that, Patty Plum ran down the road directly to the left, screaming, "Ice cream! Ice cream!" until the possum could hear her no longer.

Moments later, Peggy Plum arrived at the same fork in the road. There she was met by the very same possum. Peggy was also very anxious to reach her destination, yet when the possum began speaking, she gazed into his eyes paying close attention to every word.

"You may be wondering which direction to go,
Solve this riddle and then you will know,
Think carefully, think clearly. You must use your brain,
If you choose the wrong path, you'll be plagued by the rain,
Walk away from the darkness and into the light,
Follow the rhyme and head to the… "

Then, the possum flipped off of the tree limb and vanished into thin air.

At first, Peggy was a bit confused, but once she calmed herself down and started to think, she realized that the word "light" rhymed with "right." It was so simple! At once, she began sprinting up the right side of the path, her mouth watering and her stomach grumbling.

Hours later, Peggy arrived at a stream. She knew that she must cross it, but how? Hastily, she began searching for a large rock, a plank, or a sturdy tree limb. But her search was soon interrupted when a brilliantly colored fish ascended from the water.

"Psst," said the fish, "little Ms. Plum.
The good fairy told me that you would come.
If you head to the east where the campers set fire,
You will find a broken-down raft and a mountain of tires.
Choose one for your journey, but remember choose wise,
There are snakes in this water of gargantuan size."

And with that, just as the possum, the fish disappeared into thin air.

Quickly, Peggy ran over and examined her two choices. The top of the raft was a bit dingy, and deflated. Yet still she thought that it may float. But when she flipped it over, she noticed that a rat had gnawed away at the bottom, leaving it riddled with deep gashes and bottomless holes.

She then examined one of the tires. No holes, she thought. This will float much better. And with that she hopped onto the tire and floated across the creek in no time at all.

Moments later, Patty Plum arrived at the creek. She was soaking wet and absolutely furious. "Everyone is out to get me," she whimpered. "I just know that that fairy made it rain!"

When the fish heard her, he floated out of the water, just as he had done before. But before he could utter a word, Patty Plum grabbed the raft and wildly sprinted into the water.

For a short while, the raft remained afloat. But as time passed, Patty found herself sinking quickly into the contaminated creek.

"Stupid raft," she shouted, as she hurled the lifeless rubber mass across the water. "I can't believe that fairy left me this—this—this—thing! That is it!"

She was just about to turn back. Then, all of a sudden, out of the polluted water, an enormous snake appeared. It revealed its razor sharp fangs and let out an earth shaking "Hssss!"

At once, Patty began kicking, pushing and pulling, all while screaming out at the evil snake, "I know the fairy sent you! I know the fairy sent you!" And within seconds, she reached the other side of the creek.

Meanwhile, Patty's sister Peggy had almost arrived at the Untimely River. As she moved closer, she noticed a bright light in the distance. She followed the light until she finally reached an immense mountain of ice cream. It was just as the fairy had predicted. She pulled the fedora down over her ears, climbed to the middle of the mountain and began eating. It was a dream come true.

After about an hour or so, Peggy descended from the mountain. She noticed that the ice cream was beginning to melt and she had eaten just enough. That's when she heard screaming from across the river.

"I can't believe this stupid trip! I didn't do anything wrong and still it's ruined!"

She knew it was Patty.

Peggy looked back toward the mountain of ice cream. It was melting faster and faster! She knew that within seconds the ice cream mountain would be nothing more than a treacherous ocean of milky white waves. She motioned to her sister. "Do not cross the river! Do not cross the river!"

Ignoring her sister's warning, Patty Plum began trudging though the creek. "That's ridiculous!" she shouted. "That is just ridic—"

Just then, a huge wave of melted vanilla ice cream overpowered Patty Plum, knocking her flat onto her back. Peggy watched as her sister tried to stay afloat. At first, she could see her two straggly braids bobbing up and down between the waves. But then, after seconds of struggle, Peggy Plum saw her sister no more.

Immediately, Peggy grabbed the tire and began paddling through the waves of white chocolate. Up and down she drifted, until finally she caught sight of two straggly pigtails. She followed the strands of matted wet hair, until finally she sighted her sister, floating on top of a giant chocolate chip.

Knowing that the chocolate chip was sure to melt, Patty plunged into to the ocean of ice cream, kicking frantically until she finally reached the top of the tire.

"I can't believe it!" cried Patty, as she wiped the ice cream from her eyes. "This has been an awful day!"

Peggy shook her head and giggled. "I disagree. I think it's been rather interesting!"

As they floated past the fish and the gray-haired possum, Patty hung her head and sighed. Then she splashed a little melted ice cream on her sister and muttered, "You're just lucky. That's all."

And with that the two girls floated back to Pinkerstown, until they finally arrived back at home, in their beds, awaiting their next encounter with the good fairy.

## Discussion Points

1.  Patty Plum had trouble reaching the Untimely River. Identify two reasons why she experienced difficulty reaching the river.

2.  Peggy Plum arrived at the Untimely River before her sister Patty. Explain why Peggy arrived at the Untimely River first.

3.  Describe how Patty and Peggy acted when they each met the possum. Do you believe that one acted more appropriately than the other? Explain why.

4.  Patty chose the raft instead of a tire when crossing the creek. Identify the main reason why she chose the raft. What were the consequences of making this choice?

5.  Describe what Patty could have done differently to help her reach the mountain of ice cream sooner.

6.  Do you think that it is hard for Peggy to be sisters with Patty? Explain why or why not.

7.  Patty always blamed everyone else when she got in trouble. Discuss why this was harmful.

8.  Give reasons why the possum and the fish were more helpful to Peggy than Patty.

9.  Explain why Peggy received an ice cream reward and Patty went home hungry.

10. Tell about a time when you felt like Patty or Peggy Plum.

## Analysis

As the story indicates, Patty's impulsive behavior creates problems for her. Rather than thinking before acting or listening to the advice of others, Patty responds to situations in a hasty, out-of-control manner. Unfortunately, because she does not have the opportunity to reflect on past experiences, she does not realize that each negative consequence is a result of a negative behavior.

Throughout the story, the reader will note that Patty often blames others when faced with a negative consequence. She refers to her sister's successes as "just luck," and refuses to view the outcome as a product of her actions. This not only affects her, but also affects her sister, Peggy.

In discussing this story, encourage the child to share how Patty's behavior's affected her life and the lives of those around her. Talk about what Patty could have done differently to reach to mountain of ice cream in a timely manner. Furthermore, encourage the child to share a time when he or she felt like Patty or Peggy. Discuss how the situation could have been handled effectively.

## THE UNCONTROLLABLE SNOUT

Eddie the elephant had nothing to say.
He packed up his things and was off on his way.
His zoo mates had told him, "We've had it. Get out!
And don't you come back if you're bringing that snout!"
Poor Eddie's trunk was out of control.
He couldn't hold peanuts or slurp from a bowl.
"I just can't control it," the elephant cried.
"It flips and it flops," he said with a sigh.
"A tragedy," squealed the monkeys, "purely a shame,
That elephant is leaving quicker than he came!"
"And now he must go," cried the shiny white snail.
"He's just out of control," echoed the whale.
The zookeeper sighed. "I must let him go.
That snout," he said, "is out of control."
And so that very evening, as the monkeys settled down,
The keeper packed up Eddie and drove him out of town.

He drove him to the mountains and left him in the snow.
With nowhere left to turn and nowhere left to go,
Eddie walked for hours, through biting wind and rain,
'Til he stumbled on a city the locals called, "YOUR BRAIN."
The place was rather quiet, but just beneath some trees,
Eddie heard the banter of tiny little fleas.
"My, my," cried the fleas, "it can't be that bad.
Please tell us, Mr. Elephant, why you're so sad."
Eddie the elephant held up his snout.
"It causes me problems," he said with a pout.
"I can't keep it down; I can't keep it straight.
It's awful," he cried. "A miserable fate!"

At that very moment the head of the fleas
Extended his hand and said, "If you please!
Please stop that blubbering, put a smile on your face!
If you're looking for control, you've found the right place!"

"Yes," wailed the fleas. "The right place for sure."
The elephant replied, "Please tell me more."
"Well," said the fleas. "Here in YOUR BRAIN,
We learn how to live when we learn how to train.
People learn to listen. Animals learn to sit.
Lightbulbs learn to glisten and olives learn to pit!
"So remember," they said. "We're here to help out!
We'll train your brain if you train your snout!"

For the next couple weeks, Eddie worked hard,
Balancing peanuts on top of a card.
"Keep that nose steady! Keep that nose straight!"
The fleas all cried out as they counted to eight.
It was incredible, amazing, he was training his brain.
He practiced and practiced (even in rain).
"Don't lose your focus," shouted the fleas.
"And whatever you do, watch it. Don't sneeze!"

And after a month, he had mastered the skill
Of keeping his trunk unbelievably still.
The fleas were so happy, they made him a cake
Of moss-covered beetles and skin from a snake.
"To Eddie," they chanted. "An incredible soul
Who worked very hard to gain his control!
Who never lost focus or threw in the towel.
We salute our dear Eddie! Oh yes, sir, and how!"

For the rest of his life, Eddie lived in YOUR BRAIN.
He assisted the animals and taught them to train,
And every once in a while, just to help out,
He gave the children rides on his powerful snout.

## Discussion Points

1.  What was Eddie's problem?
2.  Have you ever felt like you couldn't control a part of your body?
3.  Why do you think Eddie was forced to leave the zoo? What types of problems do you think Eddie's trunk could have cause?
4.  How did the fleas help Eddie?
5.  What did Eddie do to train his trunk? Was it worth it?
6.  In the end, Eddie is a much happier elephant. Why do you think he is happier?
7.  What do you think you can do to help yourself control your body parts?

## Analysis

In the poem, Eddie the Elephant's lack of control causes problems for the other animals. As a result, Eddie is forced to leave the zoo. Fortunately, he stumbles upon a town called Your Brain. The town fleas encourage Eddie to begin working toward the goal of controlling his trunk.

Eddie finds that learning to control his trunk is a difficult task. Therefore, he finds himself under the direction of the fleas. They guide him in control-centered exercises, such as balancing cards on his nose. Fortunately, with much practice, Eddie finds that he is able to control his trunk much more easily. And, in the end, he becomes a confident, contributing citizen who is admired by the fleas and the children alike.

In analyzing this poem, the importance of self-control can be discussed. Explain how Eddie's lack of control affected his zoomates' perception of him. Also, address the issue of training. Discuss how learning to control your body parts can be difficult at first. However, with practice and encouragement, one can eventually learn to control oneself with ease.

# DRAGMALION

Wacky the wizard stood over his pot of boiling water, chanting, "Two eyes of a lizard, two wings of a bat, one skin of a snake and the tail of a rat, make me a dragon that snorts and breathes fire, dresses like a prince and talks like a sire."

He threw all of the ingredients into the pot: two eyes of a lizard, two wings of a bat, one skin of the snake and one tail of a rat. Then, he took a gigantic tree limb and started to stir.

The wizard's ball was only days away and Wacky had no time to waste. He had bragged to all of his friends. He had told his cousins, "I am going to create a beautiful dragon...a dragon that talks like a gentlemen and dresses like a prince."

Of course none of the other wizards believed him. Everyone knew that dragons had terrible manners. They spoke improper English, snorted when they spoke and breathed fire all over everyone.

But Wacky was going to prove them wrong. He was going to create a dragon that spoke proper English, snorted only in its sleep and always looked both ways before breathing fire. So, he found an old witch's chant at the wizardry library and decided to give it a try.

"All of the wizards at the Old Wizard Ball will see the grandest dragon of all!"

He stirred the pot three more times. Then, he spun around faster and faster until all one could see were the brilliant colors on his cape. He continued to chant these words until suddenly, with a "poof," the room filled with smoke.

Luckily, after a few minutes, the smoke began to clear. And there, in front of the wizard, sat the shadow of a large creature. Wacky closed his eyes and whispered, "Two eyes of a lizard, two wings of a bat, one skin of a snake and the tail of rat, please let this be my dragon of fire that dresses like a prince and talks like a sire."

He rubbed his eyes and opened them quickly. There in front of him, in the dim window light, sat a humongous green dragon.

"Speak, gentle dragon, speak," Wacky commanded. He could wait no longer. He knew that this dragon would speak with great brilliance. He could feel it.

The dragon looked back at Wacky, a bit confused. Then to Wacky's horror, he blurted out at the top of his lungs, "Hey, Wackster! What is up?"

Wacky was shocked! He thought he had created a dragon that spoke like a sire, followed the rules, had class—and composure—and brains! Where could he have gone wrong?

Hoping to solve the problem quickly, he ran back to the bookshelf and pulled down a book of spells. He'd try anything.

First, he tried the spell for language.

"Language wizard and witches afar, help him to speak like an almighty star!"

Then he pointed his wand at the dragon and waited patiently. But nothing happened.

So, he tried another spell and another spell and another spell. But nothing seemed to work.

By this time the dragon was bouncing up and down on the floor, making noises as if he was in a rock-and-roll band. "Wackman," sang the dragon. "What you be doin' hangin' around that crazy pot all day? It ain't doin' nothing!"

Devastated, Wacky wiped the sweat from his brow and looked into the eyes of the dragon. "Dragon," he said arrogantly. "If it ain't doin' nothin' that means that it is doing something."

The dragon of course had no idea what that meant. But instead of asking, he rather pulled back his tail, let out a uncontrolled snort and whacked the wizard in the back with his tail. "Boy, you is one funny wizard," he giggled. Then, he let out another grizzly grunt and patted Wacky again, but this time on the head.

That night, Wacky sat in his basement searching madly through his books of spells. He was at his wits end. How could he take this dragon to the wizard's ball? He couldn't even speak properly!

He wriggled about in his wizard's chair, thinking and thinking and thinking. Then, after hours of wrestling with his thoughts, he fell into a deep sleep. While he slept, he dreamt about the dragon at the wizard's ball. The dragon was blowing fire all over everyone, screaming, "This be the funnest ball I ever been at!" Meanwhile, all of the wizards were running wildly out of the ballroom howling at the top of their lungs.

When Wacky finally awoke, he made a brave decision. "My dragon," he said, "is going to learn to speak proper English. And I am still going to be the best wizard at the ball!"

He ran to the dungeon of spells and smiled at the dragon. "Dragon," he said, "how would you like to go to dragon school?"

The dragon jumped so high that he shook the floor when he came down. "School!" he shouted. "School! I be goin' to school!" Then he looked at Wacky very seriously and asked, "Hey, Wackman, when do I start?"

Seeing the small window of opportunity, Wacky grabbed a few books from his bookshelf and sat down next to the dragon

"First," he said, "you will learn how to greet people."

"Mmmmm," said the dragon. "I love to eat people."

"Not eat people," Wacky giggled, "greet people!"

Wacky the wizard spent the rest of the day teaching the dragon how to greet others, saying, "Hello, it's nice to meet you," instead of, "Hey there, what's up!" (Although, he did try to say "Hello, it's nice to eat you" a couple of times.)

Over the next few days, Wacky taught the dragon how to say "I am happy," instead of "I is happy." He also learned to say "I have no secret spider leg potion," instead of "I ain't got no secret spider leg potion."

And on the final and last day before the wizard's ball, the dragon learned to sit properly, shake tails calmly and control his overwhelming need to blow fire.

Finally, when the 21st day of the 12th month came, Wacky and his dragon were ready for the ball. Of course, not thinking clearly, Wacky sent the dragon off to dress in his finest clothes while he changed into his most brilliantly colored cape.

Almost minutes later, the dragon came out of his room dressed in his favorite baseball cap, tipped to the side of course, a holey T-shirt, and a pair of jeans that hardly even fit him. They were so big that they didn't even cover his hips!

Wacky gasped. "Dragon," he exclaimed, "I never even thought about proper clothing!"

Quickly, Wacky and the dragon rushed off to the nearest tuxedo shop. They found the perfect tuxedo. It fit the dragon splendidly. Then, they headed off to the ball.

When they arrived at the ball, Wacky shook tails with all the other dragons. "Nice to meet you," he said. "I am very happy to be here." And at the end of the evening, he walked out with a smile.

"You were a hit!" said Wacky. "How do you feel?"

The dragon thought for a second, squished up his nose and laughed. "I is happier than two dragons in a punch bowl!" Then, he winked at Wacky and the two friends giggled all the way home.

## Discussion Points

1.    Identify why Wacky was disappointed when he met his dragon.

2.    When Wacky fell asleep, he dreamed about the dragon at the ball. Tell about two things that the dragon was doing in the dream. Explain why this was a problem.

3.    In order to prepare the dragon for the ball, Wacky taught his new pet many different skills. Identify the skills that the dragon learned. Why was it important for the dragon to learn these skills?

4.    At the end of the story, Wacky tells the dragon that he was "a hit." Discuss why the dragon was "a hit."

5.    Do you believe that the dragon felt confident about himself in the end of the story? Explain why or why not.

6.    Describe a time when you or someone you know felt like Wacky or the dragon. Explain how you could have solved the problem successfully.

## Analysis

In the story, Wacky's dragon causes a potential problem. At first, the dragon proves only to be a disappointment, speaking improper English, acting impulsively, and behaving in a far from respectful manner. Fortunately, Wacky decides to train the dragon and finds that it has a great deal of potential.

The dragon learns to greet people, control his tail and curb his uncontrollable urge to breathe fire. As a result, he is rewarded when given a chance to attend the ball. After the ball, he realizes that Wacky appreciated his willingness to behave and as a result, feels a connection with his new owner.

In analyzing this story, the importance of self-image can be discussed. Explain why the dragon's primary behaviors were disappointing to Wacky. Also, address the issue of training. Discuss how learning to apply social norms is a necessity. Also, explain how self-confidence can be affected by the impact that one has on others.

# XIV. USING SCHOOL NEWSLETTERS TO EDUCATE PARENTS ON ADHD AND ITS TREATMENT

Educators and mental health professionals, particularly those who work with ADHD children, can provide much practical information that can be valuable to parents whose responsibility is to rear these difficult young people on a daily basis. At Norbel School it has been our practice to publish weekly newsletters for our parents. The purpose of these is to address various treatments, issues, and topics pertinent to understanding and rearing the ADHD child. Because our parents have commented so favorably on the helpfulness of these newsletters, a sample is presented for the reader's consideration. School counselors, psychologists, special educators, and other mental heath professionals may want to consider using such an approach in working with the parents of their ADHD children. Not only do these newsletters address the social, emotional, and behavioral aspects of ADHD, but they are helpful in conveying the most current information and stimulating discussion on this topic. Newsletters can also be a catalyst in bringing parents, educators, and mental heath professionals together for meaningful interchanges and cooperative efforts in helping our ADHD young people. The following contains an introduction and a sample of some of the newsletters that we have provided to our Norbel School parents. Many of these discuss the material which has been presented in this text. However, the topics are broken down into smaller units and focus on how this can be put into practice.

# NEWSLETTERS FOR NORBEL SCHOOL FAMILIES AND COMMUNITY

Paul Lavin, Ph.D.

•INTRODUCTION

•MANAGING THE ADHD CHILD: UNDERSTANDING THE BASICS

•MANAGING THE ADHD CHILD: POSITIVE AND NEGATIVE REINFORCEMENT

•THE APPLICATION OF BEHAVIOR PRINCIPLES

•EMOTIONAL FACTORS AND THEIR IMPACT ON THE CHILD'S BEHAVIOR

•EMOTIONAL FACTORS AND THEIR IMPACT ON ADHD: A CONTINUATION

•THE ACQUISITION OF EMPATHY

•RESTRUCTURING ERRANT THINKING: THE SECOND STEP IN HELPING ADHD CHILDREN

•THE ACQUISITION OF CONFIDENCE: HOW IMPORTANT IS THIS?

•PUNISHMENT: GOOD, BAD, OR SENSIBLE

•SOCIAL SKILLS TRAINING: IS THIS RIGHT FOR YOUR CHILD?

## INTRODUCTION

It was in the latter half of the 2001-2002 school year that I first began to write newsletters for the Norbel School Wednesday packet. Their purpose was to provide parents with psycho-educational information that could be of some value in understanding and rearing ADHD and learning disabled children. I tried to write these newsletters in such a way that ordinary, everyday parents would be able to understand and to put the principles of psychology into practice. Psychology is the study of human behavior. Its purpose is to provide us with a greater knowledge of those factors, enabling us to predict and control how people act. It made sense to me, therefore, that psychology should be presented in such a way that it could be used to improve the quality of life for everyone.

The reality is that psychology is probably the most important of all the sciences that we study. All of us, wittingly or unwittingly, put psychology into practice in almost every facet of our lives. Parents use psychology to try to influence their children to behave appropriately. Lawyers use psychology to present facts in such a way that a judge or jury will view their case in a favorable light. They know full well that the perception of the presented evidence has much to do in determining whether a client is convicted or acquitted. Salesmen use psychology to make a potential prospect aware of his or her "unmet needs." They then close the sale by convincing the prospect that their product or service can fill this void and improve the quality of his or her life. Olympic athletes use psychology to "psych out" their opponents. In their quest for "the gold," having a "mental edge" can provide them with that little bit of extra focus that leads to being on a Wheaties cereal box rather than just another forgotten participant. As we all have observed, a split second added or detracted from an athlete's score can make all the difference between glory and anonymity. A person's attitude, confidence, and having "nerves of steel" can be a big advantage when the physical ability of the participating athletes is virtually at the same level. And this is where psychology enters into the mix. This is the "mental edge" that I referred to earlier.

There are numerous examples of the daily practice of psychology ranging from a simple conversation between friends to the complex interpersonal negotiations that take place between corporate tycoons and high-ranking government officials. Whether we are aware of it or not, such interchanges are governed by the perceptions of the participants. And the forming and alteration of such perceptions have their roots in the psychological make up of the involved parties.

How powerful a knowledge of psychology can be. It not only provides us with greater self-insight and control, but it can be used to manipulate those who are inadvertently unaware of the inner forces governing their actions. A stinging word, a "politically incorrect" phrase, or a simple statement of sarcasm can drive some people "over the edge" whereas others are unaffected by such language. Why do people react so differently to the same stimulus? The answer is perception, perception, perception! And this is the province of psychology. He who understands and controls the shaping and modification of human perception has great power indeed. Great historical figures have confirmed this time after time. Their ability to influence the views of other, whether for good or evil, has had a marked impact on the unfolding of worldly events. Rightly or wrongly, it is perception that is the driving force for which men risk life and limb.

This brings me back to the purpose of the weekly newsletter. As we all know, the forming of perceptions about self and others and the development of good habits begins early in the child's life. Hopefully, these newsletters will provide you, our parents, with useful information that can be of benefit in helping your children to develop a good self-concept and the ability to cope with the many challenges that will face them now and in the future. For ADHD and learning disabled youngsters, this can be a daunting task, particularly in light of the fact that earlier repeated failures have led to the eroding of their self-confidence and spawned those accompanying negative views associated with this. However, despite their blighted past, the good news is that our children are still malleable and capable of altering their negative self-perceptions and behavioral habits. These have not become fixed personality traits that can be so stubbornly resistant and impervious to change. Arranging an appropriate environmental context and providing the proper educational tools can go a long way in repairing the damage of the past. Moreover, it can provide the child with the capability to face future challenges with confidence and optimism.

One other point is worthy of note. Some of the enclosed newsletters comment on societal issues and how these impact on us. Societal events can influence how we parent our children. Because of their significance, we often have to explain their importance to our youngsters and how to cope with the challenges that they present. Societal problems and our perceptions of them can have far-reaching implications on how we conduct ourselves and how we prepare our children in facing the present and the future. As I noted earlier, perception is the province of psychology. It makes sense, therefore, that we examine this within the broader social context as well. After all, societal events can deeply affect each and every family. How we, as parents and educators, view these can make all the difference in forming and implementing viable strategies for coping with them.

Let me end this discourse with one final thought. How we perceive things is the only facet of life over which we have absolute control. Because most of us are caught up in a daily routine, it is easy to believe that we have absolute control of the many external circumstances impacting upon our lives. We wake up each day, take our children to school, perform our daily work tasks, and get paid by our employer at the end of the week. As long as we do our part, things unfold as expected. There appears to be a direct connection between our actions and the consequences that follow. This obviously has some truth to it. However, should an untimely death, injury, unanticipated job loss (through no fault of our own), economic recession, or war occur, our best laid plans can become unraveled. And we may have done nothing to bring any of this about. It is in times like these that we recognize how limited our control happens to be.

To be sure, there may be nothing we can do about the unfair adversities that are heaped upon us. How we react to these unsolicited psychic invaders is another matter, however. We can control what we think about these annoying intruders, and we can choose a course of action (this might mean simply accepting that we cannot change things) for coping with them. Once again, this is the province of perception, the only facet of human nature over which we have true control. Yes! Psychology is a most powerful tool if it is understood and applied appropriately. As indicated earlier, psychology and the practice of it affects almost every aspect of our lives. This is what these newsletters are about. Hopefully you, our Norbel School parents, will find these to be a meaningful addition in helping you to function as a nurturer, role model, and the primary educator of your children.

# MANAGING THE ADHD CHILD:
# UNDERSTANDING THE BASICS

The parents of ADHD children frequently ask what they can do to have a greater impact on their child's behavior. They want their youngster to be more attentive, goal directed and, above all, less impulsive. The research clearly shows that good behavioral management is one of the most significant components for helping the ADHD child. However, learning to manage the child's behavior is not a simple task. It requires an understanding of human behavior, focusing upon why people act the way that they do.

Let's begin with some of the basic facts about human behavior. Behavior usually does one of three things. It increases, decreases, or stays relatively the same. This is determined by the consequences that follow the behavior. Beneficial consequences increase behavior and negative consequences decrease it. If our behavioral pattern is a stable one, this occurs because the benefits attached to it insure its continuance. We go to work every day because we receive a paycheck at the end of the week. We stop at a red light in order to avoid getting into an accident. Day after day, month after month, and year after year our behavior waxes and wanes and is maintained by such mundane consequences. In essence, these have a powerful influence on the way that we live our lives.

As parents and educators, understanding how our actions influence our child, and in turn, how the child affects us is critical. Without such insight, pandemonium can prevail. Parents and children can unintentionally become the victims of each others' behavior. For example, if you want to observe true chaos in action, I would suggest that you go to the supermarket at 4 p.m. on a Friday afternoon. Chances are that you will find some poor mother standing in a line with a full cart of groceries. Her ADHD youngster will be hanging off the side of the cart while she is anxiously waiting to exit the store. As this poor mother moves closer to the cash register, her ADHD child, who is already in impulsive overdrive, spies the candy racks in the aisle just before the register. The child, being well versed in parental manipulation, forcefully insists that he absolutely needs the colored candy with the #5 red dye in order to be happy. Mom, on the other hand, knows that giving him the candy will not only rev up his already overactive motor, but it will insure that he won't eat his supper later on.

Mom resorts to reason but this has no impact. Logic and even pleading go unheeded. Rather, junior turns up the heat. He becomes louder and more obnoxious, insisting that he must have the candy and that it won't spoil the evening meal. Mom knows that she should hold firm. However, she is caught in the middle of the line, and junior is playing a game of "uproar" at her emotional expense. Mom doesn't want to look like a mean and nasty parent. Beside, mom has a pretty good idea of what the lady behind her is thinking. "Boy, if I were in charge of that child, he would never behave like that." Mom is embarrassed, and this only worsens as junior rails on. Deep down inside, she believes that a good parent should be able to control her child. Unfortunately, the people in front and in back of her are observing first hand just how inadequate she happens to be. Mom is caught in a dilemma. She knows that if she gives in, she will feel guilty. She instinctively knows that the candy is not good for her child. However, the embarrassment and the stares from the other adults in the line are most unnerving. Mom will do almost anything to stop the pain. So what does mom do? She says to her child, "Okay. You can have the candy. But I want you to eat only one piece." By compromising, her feelings of guilt are assuaged. The "one-piece rule" at least sets some limits.

Junior grabs the candy from the rack. He opens the package and gulps down as many pieces as he can get into his mouth. He hardly pays attention to the "one-piece rule." Mom tries to rationalize away any of the guilt that she feels by telling herself that this won't happen again. But junior is quiet for now. The adults in the line stop peering at her and her embarrassment finally abates. The torture is over, at least for the moment, until she goes back to the supermarket again.

In our next newsletter we will analyze the consequences of junior's behavior in greater depth. A discussion of managing these consequences by properly applying behavioral principles will also be focused upon.

# MANAGING THE ADHD CHILD:
## POSITIVE AND NEGATIVE REINFORCEMENT

As behavior managers, let's examine last week's situation more closely. What were the consequences of junior's behavior? First, junior has learned that being loud and obnoxious, particularly in the line at the supermarket pays off. The chances are that he will behave this way again unless the consequences change. Mom has also inadvertently learned something as well. If she gives in to junior, she can escape the embarrassment that occurs in situations like this. Common sense clearly tells us that unless alterations occur, matters will only worsen, particularly when junior reaches adolescence. He will only become more impulsive and self-centered. These are hardly the traits that will endear him to others.

Parents and educators have a responsibility to try to reverse this pattern of behavior before it becomes an even more serious problem. In order to be successful in this regard, we need to understand that there are three types of consequences that largely influence the way in which we behave. Positive and negative reinforcement increase the frequency of behavior, and punishment terminates it. Positive reinforcement occurs when pleasant consequences follow a behavior. For example, a student studies hard and receives an A grade. It is more likely for the behavior to occur again, due to the "A" grade that was received by the student. Negative reinforcement occurs when behavior increases and is maintained in order to escape or avoid unpleasant consequences. For instance, an adult drives within the speed limit in order to avoid getting a ticket. A child does his homework in order to escape from mom's nagging reminders. It is important to keep in mind that both positive and negative reinforcement increase and maintain much of our ongoing daily behavior.

Punishment presents a quite different picture, however. Punishment always stops a behavior. It never increases that behavior. For example, Sammy behaves badly while the family is watching TV. His parents send him to his room to punish him. When Sammy returns, his behavior is more appropriate. Clearly, the punishment stopped Sammy's bad behavior. Therefore, sending him to his room was truly a punishment. Sammy has also learned that if he wants to avoid being sent to his room in the future, he had better be quiet and more respectful when the family is watching television. In this example, the threat of being sent to his room now becomes a negative reinforcement. Sammy's appropriate behavior increases in order to avoid losing the opportunity of watching television with the family.

Parents sometimes complain that they punish their child but that he or she continues to behave poorly. If this is so, what they think is a punishment is not viewed as such by the youngster. Punishment, in order to be effective, must be considered to be unpleasant. The child must think of it in this light if it is to have any impact in stopping an undesirable behavior. If a punishment is not working, we need to examine the results of it more closely. In the previous example, Sammy stopped behaving badly because being sent to his room was unpleasant. However, suppose that his room was filled with games, interesting books, and toys. Being sent to his room would hardly be a punishment. In all likelihood, Sammy would continue to be annoying when the family was watching television. In fact, by sending him to his room, his parents might be inadvertently rewarding him for his negative attention seeking. The punishment, in this example, would not be a punishment after all. Rather, it could be rewarding the very behavior that we are trying to terminate.

In summary, the first step in learning to be a successful behavior manager is to understand those factors that influence our child's behavior. Remember, positive and negative reinforcement account for much of why we behave in the way that we do. If these are understood and applied appropriately, we can utilize them to train our child to behave responsibly at home, in school, and in the community.

## THE APPLICATION OF BEHAVIORAL PRINCIPLES

In the last newsletter, it was emphasized that what followed a behavior determined whether that behavior continued. It was indicated that positive and negative reinforcement increased the frequency of a behavior while punishment terminated it. The proper application of reinforcement can have a profound impact on improving the ADHD child's performance. The following principles are particularly important:

1. Your child's environment should be consistently structured throughout the course of the day. From the time your child gets up in the morning until bedtime, the repetition of the same "old" behaviors should be required. Once these become a habit, they can be replaced with new behaviors. Consistency, repetition, and persistence must be emphasized. This is what improves concentration and memory and develops good habits.

2. All objects and activities, which your child finds desirable, must be earned by engaging in appropriate behavior. Keep in mind that you must distinguish between necessities and luxuries in forming this list. Luxuries are objects and activities that are not essential to your child's education, health, or well-being (e.g. junk foods, soft drinks, television, video games, recreational reading etc.). Necessities, on the other hand, are essentials that are needed for school, for proper nutrition (not necessarily pleasant tasting foods), for appropriate dress (not necessarily "brand-name" clothing, which should be earned), and for proper health. Again, it should be stressed that luxuries should be earned, not given freely.

3. Punishment, in order to be effective, must be viewed by the child as being unpleasant. The following must be kept in mind in administering punishment. First, punishment delivered by an adult who the child respects is more likely to be effective in terminating inappropriate behavior. Second, a punishment should be delivered at the onset, during, or immediately following an act in order to maximize its effectiveness. Third, if the punishment must be delayed, then it must be intense enough to offset the pleasure that preceded it. In other words, the pain or loss received later wasn't worth the pleasure gained by the earlier inappropriate behavior. Fourth, be dispassionate in administering the punishment. Give a short, not a lengthy explanation on why the

punishment was given. Avoid heated debates and "power struggles." Fifth, don't become discouraged when the child says "I don't care" following a punishment. Even though the loss might be painful, he or she is not likely to admit this. Sixth, make sure the punishment fits the crime. It must be intense enough to convince the child that the inappropriate act is not worth repeating. However, it should not be so harsh that the child becomes discouraged and gives up trying. Lastly, never follow a punishment with a display of affection. Otherwise, the child might inadvertently learn that punishment can be beneficial because it sets the stage for receiving your affection later on.

4. In setting up any behavioral program, it is important to begin rewarding successful completion of relatively easy tasks at first. Reward more difficult tasks later on. Quick beginning success makes it more likely that the child will "get hooked" into the program.

5. Both parents must agree on the required behaviors and how the program is to be implemented. Parental consistency prevents the child from "driving a wedge" between you and your spouse. Make sure that your child is not allowed to play one parent off against another.

6. Make sure that your child fully understands the expected requirements. Communicate clearly, concretely, and behaviorally with him or her. For example, say, "Sit up right in your chair. Keep both feet on the floor; and eat your food with your fork" rather than, "Be good at the table."

7. All transitions need to be planned in advance with your ADHD child. ADHD children do not adapt to change easily. Adapting to a new situation needs to be planned in advance. In this way, the child will be mentally, emotionally, and behaviorally prepared to cope with the change.

8. Break large tasks into small tasks. Reward the child for successfully completing each of the smaller tasks. This will prevent the child from becoming overly frustrated and discouraged.

9. If one of the two parents is largely responsible for rearing the ADHD child, then he or she will need relief from time to time. Periodic arrangements for "rest and relaxation" need to be made so that one can avoid becoming emotionally drained, frustrated, and overly discouraged. Help from grandparents, a support group, or the less involved parent will help one from becoming "burned out."

10. Lastly, it is important to conduct a family meeting at a specific time with your child on a daily basis. This insures that program consistency and follow through are maintained. The meeting will enable parents to reward responsible behavior and point out where improvements need to be made. Moreover, the daily meeting shows that you take the program seriously.

## EMOTIONAL FACTORS AND THEIR IMPACT ON THE CHILD'S BEHAVIOR

In our last newsletter, it was indicated that even the best behavior modification system can be undermined if the child fails to cooperate with his or her parents. As pointed out previously, emotional factors can sometimes be a major detriment to the program's effectiveness. Many ADHD youngsters have emotional problems that are secondary to or are associated with their disorder. This must be taken into account in working with them.

Being an ADHD child is not easy. His or her inattention, failure to complete assignments, and low frustration tolerance often result in a steady stream of negative feedback from parents, teachers, and peers. As a result, many ADHD children, despite being of at least average intelligence, believe that they are "stupid" and disliked by those around them. The ADHD child, therefore, becomes easily frustrated and quickly overreacts to even helpful criticism. ADHD children know that they are different. The stinging reminders of their inadequacies, even from well-meaning people, only rubs salt in the wound. And like any wounded person, they quickly strike back. Arguing, oppositional behavior, and making comments such as "I don't care" or "Whatever" are defensive maneuvers that are unconsciously produced for the purpose of protecting the little bit of self-esteem that still remains in their bruised and battered ego.

It is no wonder that many ADHD youngsters lack confidence in themselves and the people around them. They often expect to fail and to be chastised and criticized. This mental set can only leave them in a despondent, overly anxious, and resentful condition. And it is this condition that interferes with the child's ability to learn and to establish viable social relationships. In fact, this negative emotional state can actually produce and exacerbate those symptoms that are characteristic of ADHD. The child's failure to listen and to attend and his or her tendency to overreact may actually worsen. This only makes him or her appear even more willful and stubborn than usual. Such behavior elicits even more negative reactions from teachers, parents, and peers, which, in turn, keeps this never-ending counterproductive cycle going.

How do we stop this emotional merry-go-round? We must first recognize that the child's oppositional behavior is the symptom, not the cause of the problem. It is a poor self-concept and the pain of feeling inadequate that cause the child to act negatively toward us and those around him. It is important, therefore, that we respond in a different manner than that which the child would expect. As noted earlier, ADHD children often expect others to be critical and to make derogatory comments to them. Instead of chastising the child, we need to empathize with his plight, conveying that we understand why he feels frustrated. This then needs to be followed by encouraging comments indicating that we have confidence in the child's ability to perform successfully. It is important to maintain a positive tone in communicating with your ADHD child. If you allow your feelings to get hurt or become enraged by his or her sarcastic comments or stubborn reactions, you will simply be reinforcing the child's faulty notion that "everybody is against me." Responding in the opposite fashion of what the child expects and "keeping your cool" will eventually produce beneficial results. The child will come to view you as his or her advocate, not one of the "enemy." The youngster's defensiveness will gradually diminish, and he or she will become more receptive to what you have to say. Cooperativeness and improved behavior are then more likely to follow.

In the next newsletter, our discussion of emotional factors and their impact on the ADHD child's behavior will continue. Although many youngsters may exhibit ADHD symptoms, it could be that anxiety and/or depression stemming from environmental disruptions is largely responsible for these. This will be our topic for next week.

## EMOTIONAL FACTORS AND THEIR IMPACT ON ADHD: A CONTINUATION

In our last newsletter, it was indicated that emotional impediments such as chronic anxiety, depression, and anger could be responsible for the appearance of and marital or family discord can have a profoundly negative impact on the child's emotional exacerbation of ADHD symptoms. It may be that the child's continued ongoing exposure to unresolved environmental stressors is responsible for his or her failure to concentrate, to complete assignments, and to engage in impulsive, acting-out behavior. For example, young children, and even adolescents, often experience considerable affective turmoil if their parents have an acrimonious relationship or are in the process of separation or divorce. For a child, the shattering of a once intact family, no matter how dysfunctional, is a heart wrenching and painful experience. While the youngster may not talk about the emotional pain associated with this, it does not mean that he or she is unaffected by what is occurring. Rather, it is the opposite that is actually taking place.

Numerous and troubling questions run through the child's mind. Am I responsible for my parents' breakup? What could I have done to make them stay together? Will my parents still love me now that they are apart? What should I do when mom talks about dad or when dad talks about mom? Why can't my parents work this out and get back together? Who is really at fault? Should I take sides or try to remain neutral? Why do things have to be this way? These are just a few of the questions that plague the troubled child. Even when these are addressed, uncertainty, insecurity, and continued confusion associated with the breakup still remain. The hurt, anxiety, depression, and anger that the child experiences just doesn't go away that easily. Emotional turmoil and the pain accompanying it repeatedly resurrect themselves.

It is important to recognize that the child's preoccupation with family problems can become overwhelming. Carrying such an emotional burden can absorb so much psychological energy that there is little left over for learning. And how does the child behave in the face of this? He or she fails to attend; important tasks go unfinished; and excuse making, complaining, and whining become rampart. Emotionally burdened children become easily frustrated. Sometimes they become teary eyed and cry for no apparent reason. At other times they quickly become hostile and defiant, particularly when demands are placed upon them. While emotionally wrought youngsters may exhibit ADHD symptoms, their errant behavior is driven by affective rather than biochemical causes. It is imperative, therefore, that these unresolved emotional issues be addressed in working with them.

It is important to keep in mind that children are not miniature adults whose behavior is necessarily governed by logic and "right reasoning." Rather, they are emotionally fragile and can become easily undone by adverse environmental conditions. These, in essence, could actually be responsible for the child's ADHD-like symptoms and the oppositional behavior associated with them. Simply diagnosing the child with ADHD and providing medication is unlikely to resolve the problem. In fact, such an oversight could lead to continued educational and social difficulties. Addressing the child's emotional concerns, therefore, can be of the utmost importance in helping the child to make real and sustaining progress. As parents and educators, we cannot afford to overlook them.

# THE ACQUISITION OF EMPATHY:
# A FIRST STEP IN HELPING ADHD CHILDREN

Empathy is a psychological term that is battered around by educators, mental health professionals, and laypeople alike. Some people confuse empathy with sympathy, pity, or the unconditional love of another person. However, empathy is none of the preceding. Rather, it is the ability to walk in someone else's shoes. Empathy requires that we experience the internal world of another person by trying to put ourselves in his or her place. When we empathize with another human being, we can feel what that person feels, think what he thinks, and understand why he acted as he did. Empathy does not mean that we approve of someone else's behavior or that we feel sorry for him. It merely requires that we are able to perceive the world and the people in it in the same manner as that person with whom we are interacting.

While many people might believe that it is easy to empathize with others, this is far from the truth. In order to empathize, we have to be objective. This means that we must temporarily put aside our own feelings in order to try to understand those emotional, intellectual, and social factors that are motivating or driving the other person's behavioral engine. Setting aside our own feelings or disengaging from a "power struggle" in which an unreasonable youngster appears to be intentionally trying "to pluck our nerves" can be a daunting task. After all, we are adults deserving of respect. Furthermore, we are usually objectively correct when we criticize the child's errant behavior and insist that he or she make an immediate effort to correct it.

Unfortunately, logic and right reasoning have little impact on an ADHD child who is caught in the locking grip of an emotional quagmire. It is not objectivity, but the child's subjective impressions that are the propelling force behind every self-defeating action that we observe. Unless we understand this and can make a plan to correct it, there is little chance that the behavioral improvements that we seek will take place.

How many times have we interacted with an emotionally distraught youngster who is angry about some perceived injustice with a parent, a sibling, a peer, or a teacher that might have occurred several weeks or even months ago? How many times might the child have vented his or her frustration over the fact that this injustice was never recognized by those in authority and still remains uncorrected to this day? The unrelenting teasing of peers, the insensitive criticism of adults, or the blame for overreacting to the harassment of classmates is not easily forgotten. The negative affective residue of such incidents continues to be mulled over in the child's mind. These fester like an untreated cold sore that never heals. Even though the pain might be temporarily forgotten during tranquil times, it still remains deeply embedded in the unconscious recesses of the child's psyche. This becomes most readily apparent when the next power struggle emerges over an issue concerning "fairness." The youngster is quick to air out the dirty laundry from the past as a justification for his or her present overreactive behavior or rule violation.

One might ask, what does all this have to do with the importance of empathy? The answer to this question is simple enough. It is empathy that enables us to diffuse the child's excessive emotionality and helps him to put his affective life into proper perspective. The child who perceives an adult as understanding, accepting, and caring is more likely to be receptive to what that adult says to him or her. Children are much more likely to argue, to make excuses, and to react with hostility when they think we are "against" or "out to get" them. Even sincere, well-meaning adults, who actually care deeply for problem children, will fail to influence them unless they are perceived as being empathetic. That is how important empathy just happens to be. It is the primary ingredient upon which all helping relationships are built, especially those with troubled children and adolescents.

As noted earlier, empathy requires that we be objective and that we temporarily suspend our judgment about the "goodness" or "badness" of the child's actions. We must ask ourselves, "How would I feel if I were this child? How would I think if this happened to me? How would I behave if I felt and thought the same way as this youngster?" By stepping back and attempting to answer these questions, we can envision what it is like to walk in this child's shoes. Once this is accomplished, we will have acquired the trait of being empathetic. This is the key that unlocks the door to understanding those emotional demons that can fuel the fire of the ADHD child's impulsivity, inattention, and behavioral overreactions.

In order to become empathetic, it is important to construct a profile of those characteristics and situations that impact on the ADHD child and then ask ourselves how we would feel if we had to confront these. For instance, we might ask ourselves the following:

"How would I feel if...
I acted impulsively and couldn't understand why I behaved in this way?
I couldn't complete my work because I was so easily distracted?
I had to take pills because I couldn't control my behavior even when I tried?
I was constantly teased, ridiculed, and bullied by my peers?
My parents were always frustrated with me because I behaved so poorly?
My teachers always complained to my parents about my poor self-control?
I was repeatedly moved from one school or program to another because nobody was able to help me?
My parents said they "had tried everything" but they were just unable to get me to behave responsibly?
I had to see a psychiatrist for pills and a counselor because nobody understands me?
I believed that I am stupid and couldn't learn like other kids?
My siblings did well in school, had friends, and were invited places but I was left out?
I was too hyper to participate in community activities, and when I tried, the supervising adults would call my parents and complain about me because I didn't "fit in"?
I was told that I had ADHD at the age of six and that my "special needs" meant that I had to be taught differently than the other kids in my class?
I had to have extra tutoring after school because, unlike the other kids, I just don't get it the first time around?
How would I feel if these things happened to me?

The chances are that the child would feel considerable emotional pain. It would be immensely hurtful to know that he or she was not measuring up to the expectations of his or her parents and teachers. Moreover, knowing that his or her classmates considered him or her to be "stupid" would be particularly painful. The chances are that the child would be sad at best and depressed at worst. How can anyone feel good about themselves when they perform so poorly day after day?

Beside the hurt, the chances are that the child would be angry, maybe even furious. He or she did not choose to have ADHD or consciously decide to become academically and socially different. The fact that few, if any, people understand the child would cause a considerable amount of rage. The child may think, *Adults are supposed to be compassionate and guide children. Yet, all that I received were admonitions and a belly full of criticisms.* Kindness, encouragement, and patience are in short supply when you are a child conflicted with ADHD. Like any wounded soul, many ADHD children react accordingly. They are ready to be combative, even before the first words of an interchange are spoken.

Therefore, it is particularly important to learn to diffuse this pain. If this is not taken into consideration, academic growth is likely to proceed slowly at best, and the youngster's social and emotional growth will stagnate. Diffusion begins by acknowledging the child's emotional pain and giving credence to the feelings and perceptions that are responsible for these feelings. After all, anyone would be frustrated if this affliction were thrust upon them, particularly during the most youthful and promising years. Therefore, when the child is venting his or her frustration, it would be better for you, the caring adult, to verify what the child feels and why he or she feels this way. For example, a child might complain that he was unfairly sent out of the classroom for being noisy. He claims that the other children were also engaging in this kind of behavior. In a firm but soothing voice you might say, "You're really angry that the teacher put you out of the classroom for making noises. Other kids were doing the same thing and this did not happen to them. You resent being singled out by the teacher. You think that she is out to get you. And you are frustrated because you think that this is unfair and nothing is being done about it. No wonder you are angry. If I was in your shoes, I would feel the same way." (Pause). The "pause" gives the child time to integrate what you have said. This provides the youngster with the opportunity to examine his or her feelings and the perceptions responsible for them. Moreover, such a response demonstrates that you can empathize with the child's plight. Again, this increases the likelihood that he or she will be more receptive to the corrective information that is to follow. Notice that in the preceding example the helping adult did not say that the child's perception was accurate or that the youngster should not be penalized for making noises. Rather, the child's feelings and the thoughts attached to them were verified, along with an acknowledgement that, "If I viewed things in this way, I too would be frustrated."

As noted earlier, such an empathetic response helps to remove the defensiveness that interferes with one's potential to learn. It creates a more benign and receptive environment that can facilitate both the social and emotional growth within the child. After the "pause" and the calm that follows, we can then insert the pivotal words "however" or "but" which pave the way for the presentation of new information for the child's consideration. This new information will enable the child to reevaluate the problem, to correct his or her errant thinking, and to gain greater self-control. However, what follows these "pivotal words" is the subject of another newsletter.

## RESTRUCTURING ERRANT THINKING:
## THE SECOND STEP IN HELPING ADHD CHILDREN

In the previous newsletter, it was noted that empathy was the building block for establishing rapport with your ADHD child. Empathy enables us to help the child put words on his or her feelings and perceptions. Moreover, it demonstrates that we understand the ADHD youngster's plight and that we sincerely care about helping him or her. After all, even adults tend to search out persons who understand and accept them when they are confronted with a problem. We want someone whom we trust to be responsible for helping us "to work through our feelings." Children and adolescents are no different. They, too, want to be understood and to talk with persons who they believe genuinely care about them.

None of us like to be looked down upon, treated with distain, or ignored. We usually try to avoid those individuals who treat us in this fashion. In fact, such people arouse the worst feelings within us, making it very difficult to control ourselves in their presence. If maintaining emotional control is hard for adults in these circumstances, imagine how much more difficult this would be for a child or an adolescent. Because of their youth and lack of living experience, they have yet to acquire the maturity and skills for keeping "cool" in the presence of "the enemy." It's no wonder that ADHD youngsters become frustrated so easily. Again, this is why empathy is so important. It helps to diffuse this potentially emotional time bomb before it erupts into an explosion.

In the last newsletter, I referred to "however" and "but" as "pivotal words." These came after the "pause," which provided some time for your child to integrate the empathetic statements preceding it. An example of how a pivotal word might be inserted after the "pause" is as follows: "As I indicated to you, I clearly understand why you have become so frustrated. However…" It is at this point that new information can be presented for the child's consideration. It is this new information that points out the youngster's errant perceptions; how these are responsible for triggering negative emotions; and how mistaken thinking and negative affect, in combination, lead to impulsive, overreactive behavior.

In beginning this corrective process, the first step is to point out the erroneous thoughts that are contributing to the child's emotional overreactions. The trick is for you to be able to formulate such thoughts into specific words and sentences. The next step involves presenting these to the child and showing him how "what he says to himself" is responsible for his excessively negative affect. For example, if the child has a habit of saying to him or herself, "I have ADHD. This means that I am dumb and can't learn," then he or she is bound to become depressed. This thought, of which the child may or may not be even consciously aware, must be pointed out to him or her, along with the negative affect that has become attached to it. The helping adult might state, "Because you have ADHD, you believe that you are dumb and can't learn. No wonder you are down in the dumps much of the time." After stating this, the adult might ask, "What do you think about what I have just said? Do you understand that what you think about yourself influences how you feel?" If the child is confused, further explanations can be given until the connection between errant thought and negative emotions is made.

Once the preceding is accomplished, the second step would be to present a more accurate perception that might be incorporated into the child's thinking. For example, the adult might say, "Because you have ADHD doesn't mean that you are dumb and can't learn. In fact, ADHD children are just as smart as their classmates. Having ADHD really means that you have more energy than most people. Having more energy is a good thing. If it is used properly, it means that you could actually accomplish more than many other children. You have the brain power to be successful. Your problem is learning how to properly direct and control your energy so that you can achieve this goal." This explanation helps to replace the child's errant thought with a more accurate and realistic perception of the problem. After it is presented again, asking what he thinks about your explanation will verify whether or not he has grasped the concept. If further explanation is needed, it can be provided at this point. Once the new information is integrated into the child's thinking, his or her emotional state will be altered. Instead of feeling depressed, a sense of hopefulness should arise. This, then, would serve as a catalyst for exploring strategies on how the ADHD youngster's energy might be better directed and controlled. Moreover, this approach is more likely to foster a solid rapport between you and your child, enabling you to have a much greater impact in improving the quality of his or her life.

Of course, one of the tricks in effectively implementing the preceding is to be able to recognize and to put into words those errant thoughts that are particularly problematic for children and adolescents. The ability to undertake a more productive thought pattern must then be adopted. Becoming skilled in both of these dimensions is essential in making this approach work for you. How to accomplish will be the subject of the next newsletter.

## THE ACQUISITION OF CONFIDENCE: HOW IMPORTANT IS THIS?

In an article entitled *If at First You Don't Succeed* by Janet Polivy and C. Peter Herman (*American Psychologist*, September, 2002), the authors address the importance of confidence in achieving success. These authors cited several examples of current research that was conducted between the years of 1995 and 1999. The results clearly indicated that higher self-efficacy or confidence in oneself made all the difference between success and failure. In summing up their conclusions, Polivy and Herman stated: "People who believe that they can succeed are more likely to succeed than people who do not. For one thing, those who believe in themselves are more likely to make the effort in the first place. Second, the confident individual is more likely to persist in the face of obstacles. To the extent that persistence helps the individual to overcome these obstacles, then confidence is critical to success. Indeed, there is substantial evidence that higher self-efficacy scores and confidence are associated with better outcomes in a variety of programs."

There is little doubt that belief in oneself is one of the central ingredients upon which human motivation is founded. If a person has confidence, then he or she is more likely to exert the effort to achieve desirable goals. On the other hand, should the person perceive himself as being incapable of reaching these goals, than little or no effort would be put forth. Rather, by directing one's energy into areas in which one believes, achievement would be much more likely to occur.

Let's put the preceding into a more practical context with our own children. All of us want our young people to pursue goals that prepare them to be viable, upright adult members of the community. The pursuit of a good education, the acquisition of recognition for successful achievement in the arts, sciences, and humanities and the development of athletic skills are areas in which we would like to see our youngsters to excel. Building strong work habits, developing hands on technical and mechanical competence, and learning social skills for appropriately interfacing with other people are also laudable goals that we want our children to reach in their most formative years. However, whether our young people are willing to put forth the necessary energy to achieve these goals depends primarily on how they perceive themselves and their ability to accomplish such goals. If a child believes that he is a "loser," a "retard," or just plain "dumb," he is unlikely to try to achieve any of the above. The pursuit of these goals, at least in the child's mind, requires too much time, energy, and persistence. And from the child's point of view, he believes that his efforts would hardly be successful anyway. So what's the point of trying? Why would he or she want to make life more difficult than it already happens to be? It would make more sense, therefore, to pursue more immediate goals, even if these were considered to be undesirable from the "adult point of view."

For example, most young people and adults want to be recognized by their peers for being "good" at something. Unfortunately, some children have already given up on the idea that they could ever achieve positive recognition from their parents and teachers. As a result, they take great pride in becoming antagonists. They behave rebelliously in the face of adult authority, and they mock the educational processes by becoming class clowns and social misfits. While such behavior is perceived as being counterproductive from the adult perspective, the antagonistic youngster views this quite differently. To him, being "bad" is good. Why? The answer to this is quite simple. The antagonist is often recognized as being humorous and even "cool" by his agemates. Peers laugh at the youngster's jibes at the classroom teacher. His bravado and contempt of authority are worn like badges of courage for all to see. Some secretly admire the antagonist's twisted notion of bravery, even though they would hardly dare to engage in such outrageous behavior themselves. They clearly recognize that they would have too much to lose by behaving so badly. However, deep down inside many really admire the "rebel without a cause," and they wish that they could be like him. After all, being perceived as being "cool" and "in control" is an attractive quality to a child or adolescent. And all of this recognition can be acquired almost instantly. One does not have to engage in long periods of hard work or give up the short-term pleasures that can make life so much fun for the present moment. This is what makes outrageous behavior so attractive. It can lead to immediately beneficial effects, and it requires very little substantial effort. The child or adolescent simply has to behave in an obnoxious fashion, and for some, this is a relatively easy task.

While there are many reasons (some people would call these excuses) why youngsters engage in self-defeating behavior, the root of the problem often stems from a lack of confidence in themselves. Rather than take the risk of competing against others or looking foolish, they engage in antisocial acts and gravitate toward those activities that provide them with immediate and often sensual pleasure. This lack of faith in themselves, in other people, and in life itself is like a cancer. If left untreated, it devours the living cells of an otherwise potentially good and viable personality.

If we think about the preceding, this has far-reaching implications in determining the kinds of habits and traits that become deeply embedded into our personality structure with the passage of time. People who lack confidence are much more likely "to grab the brass ring now." Even though brass tarnishes quickly and leaves a circular green stain on one's finger, the brass ring glitters at least for a moment. Bad habits are like the glittering brass ring. Whether it is drug or alcohol abuse, promiscuity, overeating, or the explosive reactions to minor irritants, these provide one with immediate and intense pleasure, relief, or temporary satisfaction. And there is one thing of which we can be certain. Such maladaptive behavior patterns do not simply come about by chance. There are causes that bring these about. The trick is to identify and to gain conscious control of them so that we can live more productive and happier lives. A lack of self-confidence is one of these major causes.

Most assuredly, the genesis of many of our adult problems began in childhood. Dashed hopes, broken dreams, and the loss of believing that our sustained efforts could ever amount to anything may have plagued many of us during our youthful years. A lack of self-confidence may have caused some of us to sell ourselves short. As a result, we might have made poor choices that now have a profoundly negative impact on the way that we are living our lives today. How many times have we heard older people say, "I'd love to live my life over again with what I know today." It is sad but true. The reality is that many adults discover potentials within themselves that, if these had been recognized and nurtured earlier, could have led to a much more satisfying and fulfilling life. However, during their most formative years their belief in themselves just wasn't there. Instead, a twisted and jaded version of who they were and what they could achieve led to "grabbing the brass ring" too early in their tumultuous youthful years.

So the question still remains. Just how important is the acquisition of self-confidence? The psychological literature and our practical observations would indicate that it is probably the most important aspect of the child's developing personality. No matter how talented a person might be, the actualization of that talent will not occur if he or she lacks the confidence to develop it. The development of self-confidence must be undertaken during the youngster's most formative years before the challenges of living become increasingly more complex and compelling. For the parents of ADHD and learning disabled children, fostering the development of confidence should not be left to chance. Our ADHD and learning disabled youngsters are particularly vulnerable in this regard. They are more likely than most of their peers to lack belief in themselves. Therefore, it is important that we attempt to correct this deficiency as soon as possible. How we might bring this about will be the subject of another newsletter.

## PUNISHMENT: GOOD, BAD, OR SENSIBLE

It has come to my attention that some parents have reservations about the term "punishment" and its applicability in modifying behavior. This, in light of the current times, is understandable. Many of us have grown up with the idea that punishment is something that is harsh and humiliating. Some perceive punishment as an "evil" to be avoided, particularly when it comes to child rearing. Unfortunately, those acts such as screaming at a child, beating him or her with a leather strap, or subjecting him or her to long periods of isolation have become associated with punishment. It is no wonder that punishment has such an abhorrent reputation. It has been administered carelessly and cruelly throughout the course of history.

Despite this, however, punishment should be an important part of our child-rearing plan. We need to reexamine punishment and more accurately assess how it can be effectively put into practice. Even though punishment is aversive, it is actually a form of discipline. Punishment involves the imposing of a penalty for violating a rule, failing to fulfill an obligation, or infringing upon the rights of another person. A penalty has three purposes: (1) to stop the child's undesirable behavior; (2) to make it less likely that he or she will engage in this behavior in the future; and (3) to require that the child make restitution to those persons who have been inconvenienced or violated by his or her behavior.

Let me give an example on how this would be put into practice. Jim steals an item from the neighborhood store. You discover the theft and confront him. You take Jim back to the store so that he can pay for or return the item. You also make Jim apologize for his behavior. Moreover, because he has inconvenienced you and violated the rights of the store owner, he is also required to perform some work-related service for the disruption that he has caused.

The consequences of Jim's behavior are all unpleasant. First, Jim receives your disapproval. Second, he has to return the item and apologize to the owner. This is embarrassing. And third, Jim has to use his free time to engage in a work-related service for the disruption that he created. Although the consequences following Jim's behavior are unpleasant, they are certainly not harsh or excessively punitive. Rather, they are appropriate for the offense that Jim has committed. In other words, "the punishment fits the crime." Unless Jim has emotional problems of a serious nature, he is likely to learn from this mistake and refrain from any future stealing.

It should be noted that the term punishment has been used in the literature on behavior modification since its inception. Punishment is a scientific term. Its purpose is to provide a label for a specific factor or event that influences the way in which we behave. Punishment, therefore, is actually neutral. Unfortunately, it often evokes strongly negative feelings in those of us that have been exposed to its worst elements. A stimulus or event only becomes a punishment when it is unpleasant enough to cause some particular behavior to stop. This is a fact that has been demonstrated empirically. Moreover, the results of punishment are evident to all of us in our ordinary everyday encounters of living.

Whether a punishment is harmful or not depends largely on the intentions and skill of the person who is applying it. Even physical punishment, if applied properly, can be beneficial. For instance, suppose that your toddler insists on trying to stick paper clips, pins, or other forms of paraphernalia into your electrical outlets. You have used your best distraction techniques, moved the furniture, and tried covering the outlets. The child undauntedly, however, continues to stick objects and even his fingers into the sockets. Would not a swat on the child's bottom accompanied by a firm NO! be appropriate? If the pain associated with the swat stopped this dangerous behavior, wouldn't the punishment have served a good purpose?

Notice that I have used the word "swat" to describe the action to be taken in this case. Beating the child until he is "beet red," screaming at or violently chastising him, or locking him in the closet for the day would hardly be appropriate. Like the swat, these would probably stop the behavior. However, such volatile overreactions would produce emotional scars within the child that might take years to heal. While a parent might temporarily alleviate his or her frustration in trying to discipline the child, these punitive measures would do more harm than good. The proper use of punishment should facilitate the child's social, emotional, and moral development. It should not impede it.

While I would hardly advocate the use of physical punishment, believe it or not, there are times when it might be absolutely necessary. For example, many educators and mental health professionals have been trained in the use of physical restraint. There are moments when reasoning will just not work with a rampaging child who may be a threat to self or others. However, physically subduing the youngster can lead to the immediate suppression of this behavior. A period of calmness can then follow. Once this occurs, addressing the problem in a rational manner can be undertaken.

Again, in this example, the proper application of restraint is utilized. This means applying minimal force for the purpose of stopping the errant behavior. It does not mean beating the child senseless, breaking one of his or her limbs, or inflicting immense physical pain in order to obtain revenge. Rather, the objective is to stop the child's potentially dangerous activity so that we can explore better ways to cope with the problem.

As one can see even physical punishment, if administered with the right intentions and properly applied, can be a humane approach for helping troubled children. Like any psychological tool, however, its effectiveness is largely determined by the motives and skills of those who use it.

The use of physical punishment (which, by the way, is referred to as "positive punishment" in psychological jargon) is usually "the court of last resort" for most of us. We would prefer to rely on what psychologists call "negative punishment." Negative punishment is actually not so negative. It means taking away something from the child when he or she behaves badly.

There are two forms of negative punishment, time-out and response cost. In the former, the child is isolated to a room by him or herself for a specified period of time following an inappropriate behavior. For instance, Mary might be sent to her room for 10 minutes after arguing with Mom. In response cost, some privilege is taken away if the child behaves inappropriately. For example, Robert might lose 15 minutes off his bedtime for each cuss word that he utters. Like physical punishment, the consequences of time-out and response cost are unpleasant. However, these approaches to discipline are more palatable to us because no actual physical pain is inflicted on the child. But time-out and response cost can also be poorly administered and harshly applied as well. For example, we can lock a child in a room for excessively long periods of time, or we can take away a child's privileges without the opportunity to earn them back within a reasonable time limit. Such excessiveness only causes the child to become despairing and can actually lead to serious withdrawal or acting out.

In conclusion, it is important to recognize that the proper use of punishment can be of the outmost importance in helping our children. The proper use of punishment can help a child to gain insight into the consequences of his or her actions. Moreover, it can enhance his or her understanding of right and wrong and how their behavior affects other people. Remember, punishment is a neutral term that simply identifies the effect that a particular stimulus or event has on a child's behavior. Whether the results of punishment are good or bad are largely determined by how we use it. Punishment can have a profound and immediate impact in stopping inappropriate behavior. However, it does have its limitations. If improperly applied, it can leave the child with emotional scars and lead to depression, withdrawal, and further acting out. It should be kept in mind that punishment teaches the child what he or she should NOT do. It does not instruct the child on how to cope with problems or in what constitutes proper behavior. This is why the application of punishment needs to be used in conjunction with the BEHAVIOR CHART that was discussed in our previous newsletters. The two approaches together make up a complete behavior modification program.

## SOCIAL SKILLS TRAINING:
## IS THIS RIGHT FOR YOUR CHILD?

It's IEP time. Parents, legal advocates, and educational professionals will be attempting to hammer out next year's individual educational program for helping your ADHD child. As we all know, ADHD children often have marked difficulty getting along with their peers. In order to remedy this, a social skills intervention program might be recommended. It is assumed that this will serve as a panacea for the child's interactive problems.

When a child fails to get along with others, it is tempting to believe that he or she does not know how to interact appropriately. The problem, therefore, is perceived as being a cognitive deficit. We assume that if we fill this void by teaching the child how to behave socially, then this "knowledge gap" will be bridged and appropriate behavior will follow. In other words, once the child knows those verbal and non-verbal behaviors that are socially appropriate, it is assumed that he or she will automatically put these into practice. After all, all ADHD children want to have friends. So obviously, the preceding rationale makes sense.

Unfortunately, more often than not, things do not work out this way. Children can be trained to use the proper social interventions by skilled educational and mental health professionals. As a result, they may then be cognitively aware of the proper response for coping effectively with varied social situations. In fact, if you ask such children how they should behave, they can tell you in detail what they should do and say. However, for many youngsters, the problem is not a lack of knowledge. Rather, it is the failure to put into practice what they know when the circumstances present themselves.

For example, Tim has trouble coping with teasing. When his peers make fun of him, he overreacts by whining, crying, and arguing with them. Tim is told to walk away; tell the teacher; or to simply ignore the teasing. He may even be told that the teasing occurs because of the way that he reacts to it. Tim might be taught to restructure his thinking and to engage in various strategies so that he can cope more effectively. However, when Tim is teased, he fails to put into practice what he has learned. Rather, he continues to behave badly when the teasing occurs.

After the fact, Tim is able to describe what he should have done. He can tell you in detail how he should have acted. However, he just didn't do it!

Why does this occur, we might ask ourselves. What is it that prevents a child who knows what he or she should do from putting this into practice, particularly when the chips are down? If we examine this more closely, there are several reasons that might account for this. First and foremost is the fact that ADHD children often have a poor self-concept, accompanied by a low frustration tolerance. Because their feelings are easily hurt, they quickly overreact to even the slightest indication of peer disrespect. Their reaction is a deeply ingrained pattern of behavior that is not easily altered, particularly when stressful circumstances arise. Rather, when the child feels pressured, he or she quickly reverts back to his or her old overreactive habits. So with great frequency, a lack of knowledge is not the problem. The child's failure to utilize what he or she knows is at the root of the difficulty.

In the April 2002 edition of *Attention*, a magazine published by the CHADD organization, it was reported that, "Although many social skills interventions for children exist, few have shown lasting change." Given this fact, it would seem prudent that our thinking about the efficacy of social skills training be reconsidered. Perhaps it would be wiser to examine the emotional state of each of our children before this recommendation is made. As noted in an earlier newsletter, the ADHD youngster must be emotionally ready to receive and integrate that which we teach. The learning of social skills, no matter how well presented, is unlikely to occur if the proper foundation has not been laid. Moreover, even if the child does learn these skills, they are not likely to be utilized if the child has a poor self-concept and becomes easily frustrated. Unfortunately, such a youngster will not have the self-control to put these into practice. As a result, the same old negative behavior patterns will persist, despite the fact that a social skills training program has been implemented.

In light of the preceding, therefore, it might be more prudent to request intensive individual, rather than a group counseling intervention for your child. Keep in mind that your child must be cognitive and emotionally ready to profit from any educational or mental health approach that is put into an IEP. It is not uncommon for ADHD children to receive social skills training that minimally impacts on the quality of their peer relationships. Make sure that such an approach is right for your child before it becomes part of your plan.

# XV. CONCLUSIONS

As the preceding clearly indicates, a multi-faceted approach is needed in order to successfully manage and treat the ADHD child. ADHD is a condition that can have a significantly negative impact, not only on the child's present level of functioning, but on his or her future performance. While ADHD is considered to be a behavioral disorder, it can have a profoundly adverse effect on the youngster's self-concept, social development, and educational functioning. Untreated or under-treated (often only with medication), ADHD children are at high risk for continued failure. With much frequency, these unfortunate young people experience learning difficulties and are afflicted with secondary emotional problems (anxiety, depression, etc.) as well. Unless these issues are addressed and treated in a forthright and direct manner, the ADHD child will continue to flounder and his or her difficulties will only worsen with the passage of time. When the youngster reaches his or her teenage years, negative behavioral habits and counterproductive thinking can become so deeply ingrained that positive changes can occur only under the most intense treatment conditions. Further, by this time, other behavioral disorders of a more oppositional nature may have become superimposed on the child's ADHD. This can make the youngster even more resistant to change even when the best and most well-meaning people try to be of assistance.

The preceding only reinforces the point that was made at the beginning of this book. If we construct good behaviorally based management programs and properly apply these during the child's most formative years, then he or she is more likely to learn to concentrate, stay on task, and control his or her impulsivity. Moreover, by teaching the youngster to alter his or her negative views during the most malleable years, better emotional control, a more positive self-concept, and improved coping skills are more likely to be acquired. This then leads to the development of an "internal locus of control," the internalized belief that one is responsible for his or her own actions and the consequences that follow. As noted earlier, it is this core belief that is the foundation upon which success is built.

Lastly, it needs to be emphasized that putting these recommended programs into practice is not an easy "quick-fix" process. Unlike medication, which usually produces an immediate calming effect, behavior modification, cognitive restructuring, self-control training, and our other recommended interventions take time, patience, and diligence. Devising "tight" behavioral programs, administering them, and troubleshooting when problems arise can be an intellectually and emotionally draining task. Building good work habits, social skills, and desirable character traits is a tough row to hoe, particularly with an ADHD child who seems intent on bucking and twisting against us at every turn. Despite this, however, success can be obtained if we are equally persistent in the pursuit and achievement of our own goals for our ADHD children.

Good child rearing is one of the most formidable tasks that parents of ADHD children can ever undertake. Those parents who are willing to go the extra mile are deserving of our utmost respect. In light of this, therefore, it is to our Norbel School parents and those who are like them that we dedicate this book.

# REFERENCES

American Psychiatric Association. (1994). Diagnostic and statistical manual of mental disorders (4th ed.). Washington, DC: Author.

Bandura, A. (1977). Social learning theory. Englewood Cliffs, NJ: Prentice-Hall.

Barkley, R. (1990). Attention deficit hyperactivity disorder: A handbook for diagnosis and treatment. New York: Guilford.

Byrd, D.P. & Byrd, K.E. (1986). Drugs, academic achievement and hyperactive children. The School Counselor, 23, 323-331.

Cotugo, A.L. (1995). Personality attributes of attention deficit hyperactivity disorder (ADHD) using the Rorschach ink blot test. Journal of Clinical Psychology, 51, 554-561.

Crandall, V., Katkovski, W. & Crandall, V.J. (1965). Children's beliefs in their own control of reinforcements in intellectual-academic situations. Child Development, 36, 90-109.

Dweck, C.S. (1975). The role of expectations and attributions in the alleviation of learned helplessness. Journal of Personality and Social Psychology, 31, 674-685.

Erk, R.R. (2000). Five frameworks for increasing understanding and effective treatment of attention-deficit / hyperactivity disorder: Predominately inattentive type. Journal of Counseling & Development, 78, 389-399.

Erk, R.R. (1995). The conundrum of attention deficit disorder. Journal of Mental Health Counseling, 17, 131-145.

Erk, R.R. (1997). Multidimensional treatment of attention deficit disorder: A family oriented approach. Journal of Mental Health Counseling, 19, 3-22.

Fry, P.S. (1975). Affect and resistance to temptation. Developmental Psychology, 11, 466-472.

Gagne, E. (1975). The effects of locus of control and goal setting on persistence at a learning task. Child Study Journal, 5, 193-199.

Goldstein S. & Goldstein, M. (1990). Managing attention disorders in children. New York: John Wiley & Sons.

Gomez, K.M. & Cole, C.L. (1991). Attention-deficit hyperactivity disorder: A review of treatment alternatives. Elementary School Guidance and Counseling, 26, 106-114.

Grenshaw, F. & Elliott, S. (1984). Assessment and classification of children's social skills: A review of methods and issues. School Psychology Review, 13, 292-300.

Hartig, M. & Kanfer, F.H. (1973). The role of verbal instruction in children's resistance to temptation. Journal of Personality and Social Psychology, 25, 259-267.

Henker, B., Walen, C. & Hinshaw, S. (1980). The attributional context of cognitive motivational strategies. Exceptional Educational Quarterly, 1, 17-30.

Kaufman, K.F. & O'Leary, K.D. (1972). Reward, cost and self-evaluation procedures for disruptive adolescents in a psychiatric hospital school. Journal of Applied Behavior Analysis, 5, 293-309.

Lambert, M.J. & Cattani-Thompson, K. (1996). Current findings regarding the effectiveness of counseling: Implications for practice. Journal of Counseling & Development, 74, 601-608.

Lavin, P. (1989). Parenting the over-active child: Alternatives to drug therapy. Lanham, MD: Madison Books.

Lavin, P. (1991). Teaching kids to think straight. Columbia, MO: Hawthorne.

Lavin, P. (1991) The counselor as consultant-coordinator for children with attention deficit hyperactivity disorder. Elementary School guidance and Counseling, 26, 115-120.

Lavin, P. (2002). Cognitive restructuring: A counseling approach for improving the ADHD child's self-concept. Dimensions of Counseling, 30, 22-27.

Lavin, P. (2003). Response cost: A home system for modifying the ADHD child's behavior. Dimensions of Counseling, 31, 25-30.

Licht, B.G., Kistner, J.A., Ozkaragoz, T., Shapiro, S. & Clausen, L. (1986). Causal attributions of learning disabled children: Individual differences and their implications for persistence. Journal of Educational Psychology, 77, 208-216.

Liebert, R.M. & Nelson, R. (1981). Developmental Psychology. Englewood Cliffs, NJ: Prentice-Hall, 422-423.

Linn, R.T. & Hodge, G.K. (1982). Locus of control in childhood hyperactivity. Journal of Consulting and Clinical Psychology, 50, 592-593.

McConnell, S. & Odom, S. (1986). Sociometrics: Peer referenced measures and the assessment of social competence. In P. Strain, M. Gurainick, & H.M. Walker (Eds.), Children's social behavior: Development, assessment and modification. New York: Academic Press.

McGuiness, D. (1985). When children don't learn. New York: Basic Books.

Meichenbaum, D. (1977). Cognitive-behavior modification. New York: Plenum Press.

Rapoport, M.D., Murphy, H.A. & Bailey, J.S. (1982). Ritalin vs. response-cost in the control of hyperactive children: A within-subject comparison. Journal of Applied Behavior Analysis, 15, 205-216.

Rapoport, M.D. (1987). The attention training system. DeWitt, NY: The Gordon Systems.

Reid, M.K. & Borkowski, J.G. (1987). Causal attributions of hyperactive children: Implications for teaching strategies and self-control. Journal of Educational Psychology, 79, 206-307.

Rosenbaum, M. & Baker, E. (1984). Self-control in hyperactive and non-hyperactive children. Journal of Abnormal Child Psychology, 12, 303-331.

Seligman, L. (1975). Helplessness. San Francisco, CA: Freeman.

Walen, C.K. & Henker, B. (1976). Psychostimulants and children: A review and analysis. Psychological Bulletin, 83, 1113-1130.

Weiner, B. (1979). A theory of motivation for some classroom experiences. Journal of Educational Psychology, 71, 3-25.

Printed in the United States
38939LVS00004BA/124

9 781413 775785